GREEK TRAGEDIES

VOLUME 2

T0056068

AESCHYLUS

The Libation Bearers Translated by Richmond Lattimore

SOPHOCLES

Electra Translated by David Grene

EURIPIDES

Iphigenia among the Taurians Translated by Anne Carson

Electra Translated by Emily Townsend Vermeule

The Trojan Women Translated by Richmond Lattimore

Edited by David Grene & Richmond Lattimore

THIRD EDITION *Edited by Mark Griffith & Glenn W. Most*

GREEK VOLUME 2
TRAGEDIES

The University of Chicago Press CHICAGO & LONDON

MARK GRIFFITH is professor of classics and of theater, dance, and performance studies at the University of California, Berkeley.

GLENN W. MOST is professor of ancient Greek at the Scuola Normale Superiore at Pisa and a visiting member of the Committee on Social Thought at the University of Chicago.

DAVID GRENE (1913–2002) taught classics for many years at the University of Chicago.

RICHMOND LATTIMORE (1906–1984), professor of Greek at Bryn Mawr College, was a poet and translator best known for his translations of the Greek classics, especially his versions of the *Iliad* and the *Odyssey*.

The University of Chicago Press, Chicago 60637
The University of Chicago Press, Ltd., London
© 2013 by The University of Chicago

The Libation Bearers © 1953, 2013 by the University of Chicago
Sophocles, *Electra* © 1957, 2013 by the University of Chicago
Iphigenia among the Taurians © 2013 by Anne Carson
Euripides, *Electra* © 1959, 2013 by the University of Chicago
The Trojan Women © 1947 by the Dial Press; © 1958, 2013 by the University of Chicago

All rights reserved. Published 2013.
Printed in the United States of America

22 21 20 19 18 17 16 15 14 13   1 2 3 4 5

ISBN-13: 978-0-226-03545-1 (cloth)
ISBN-13: 978-0-226-03559-8 (paper)
ISBN-13: 978-0-226-03562-8 (e-book)

Library of Congress Cataloging-in-Publication Data

Greek tragedies / edited by David Grene and Richmond Lattimore. — Third edition / edited by Mark Griffith and Glenn W. Most.
    pages. cm.
        ISBN 978-0-226-03514-7 (cloth : alk. paper) — ISBN 978-0-226-03528-4 (pbk. : alk. paper) — ISBN 978-0-226-03531-4 (e-book) — ISBN 978-0-226-03545-1 (cloth : alk. paper) — ISBN 978-0-226-03559-8 (pbk. : alk. paper) — ISBN 978-0-226-03562-8 (e-book) — ISBN 978-0-226-03576-5 (cloth : alk. paper) — ISBN 978-0-226-03593-2 (pbk. : alk. paper) — ISBN 978-0-226-03609-0 (e-book) 1. Greek drama (Tragedy) I. Grene, David. II. Lattimore, Richmond, 1906–1984. III. Wyckoff, Elizabeth, 1915– IV. Most, Glenn W. V. Griffith, Mark (Classicist) VI. Sophocles. Antigone. English. 2013. VII. Sophocles. Oedipus Rex. English. 2013. VIII. Aeschylus. Agamemnon. English. 2013. IX. Aeschylus. Prometheus bound. English. 2013. X. Euripides. Hippolytus. English. 2013.
        PA3626.A2G57 2013
        882′.0108—dc23

                                        2012044399

⊗ This paper meets the requirements of ANSI/NISO Z39.48–1992 (Permanence of Paper).

CONTENTS

THE LIBATION BEARERS

AESCHYLUS
Translated by Richmond Lattimore

ror comes upon him and his mind sees the Furies of his mother (the Erinyes, or Eumenides), who pursue him from the stage. The story of this pursuit and the eventual release of Orestes is told in *The Eumenides*.

All three dramatists have made the murders be accomplished by deception. Orestes presents himself disguised and is not recognized at first by his mother and her husband. In Aeschylus, the intrigue is reduced to its simplest terms. Much of the tragedy's force comes from the spellbinding rhythms and imagery of the invocation and the choral odes.

THE LIBATION BEARERS

Characters   ORESTES, son of Agamemnon and Clytaemestra
PYLADES, his friend
ELECTRA, his sister
CHORUS of Asian serving-women
A SERVANT (doorkeeper)
CLYTAEMESTRA, queen of Argos; now wife
of Aegisthus
THE NURSE, Cilissa
AEGISTHUS, now king of Argos
A FOLLOWER of Aegisthus

Scene: Argos, in front of the palace.

(Enter Orestes and Pylades, from the side.)

ORESTES
Hermes, lord of the dead, you who watch over the powers
of my fathers, be my savior and stand by my claim.°
Here is my own soil that I walk. I have come home;
and by this mounded gravebank I invoke my father
to hear, to listen.   5
He met his end in violence through a woman's treacherous
   tricks . . .
Here is a lock of hair for Inachus, who made
me grow to manhood. Here a strand to mark my grief.
I was not by, my father, to mourn for your death
nor stretched my hand out when they took your corpse away.

(Enter the Chorus, with Electra, from the other side.)

But what can this mean that I see, this group that comes   10
of women veiled in dignities of black? At what
sudden occurrence can I guess? Is this some new
wound struck into our house? I think they bring these urns
to pour, in my father's honor, to appease the powers
below. Can I be right? Surely, I think I see   15
Electra, my own sister, walk in bitter show
of mourning. Zeus, Zeus, grant me vengeance for my father's
murder. Stand and fight beside me, of your grace.
Pylades, stand we out of their way. So may I learn
the meaning of these women; what their prayer would ask.   20

(Orestes and Pylades conceal themselves, to one side.)

CHORUS [*singing*]

STROPHE A

I came in haste out of the house
to carry libations, hurt by the hard stroke of hands.
My cheek shows bright, ripped in the bloody furrows
of nails gashing the skin.   25
This is my life: to feed the heart on hard-drawn breath.
And in my grief, with splitting weft
of ragtorn linen across my heart's
brave show of robes
came sound of my hands' strokes   30
in sorrows whence smiles are fled.

ANTISTROPHE A

Terror, the dream diviner of
this house, belled clear, shuddered the skin, blew wrath
from sleep, a cry in night's obscure watches,
a voice of fear deep in the house,   35
dropping deadweight in women's inner chambers.
And they who read the dream meanings
and spoke under guarantee of god
told how under earth

dead men held a grudge still   40
and smoldered at their murderers.

On such grace without grace, evil's turning aside
(Earth, Earth, kind mother!)
bent, the godless woman   45
sends me forth. But terror
is on me for this word let fall.
What can wash off the blood once spilled upon the ground?
O hearth soaked in sorrow,
O wreckage of a fallen house.   50
Sunless and where men fear to walk
the mists huddle upon this house
where the high lords have perished.

The pride not to be warred with, fought with, not to be beaten down   55
of old, sounded in all men's
ears, in all hearts sounded,
has shrunk away. A man
goes in fear. High fortune,
this in man's eyes is god and more than god is this.   60
But, as a beam balances, so
sudden disasters wait, to strike
some in the brightness, some in gloom
of half dark in their elder time.
Desperate night holds others.   65

Through too much glut of blood drunk by our fostering ground
the vengeful gore is caked and hard, will not drain through.
The deep-run ruin carries away
the man of guilt. Swarming infection boils within.   70 .

For one who assaults the bride's pure bed, there is no cure.
All the world's waters running in a single drift

may try to wash blood from the hand
of the stained man; they only bring new blood guilt on.

But as for me: gods have forced on my city   75
resisted fate. From our fathers' houses
they led us here, to take the lot of slaves.
And mine it is to wrench my will, and consent
to their commands, right or wrong,
to beat down my edged hate.   80
And yet under veils I weep
the futile destinies of
my lord; and freeze with sorrow in the secret heart.

ELECTRA

Attendant women, who order our house, since you
are with me in this supplication and escort   85
me here, be also my advisors in this rite.
What shall I say, as I pour out these outpourings
of sorrow? How say the good word, how make my prayer
to my father? Shall I say I bring it to the man
beloved, from a loving wife, and mean my mother? I   90
have not the daring to say this, nor know what else
to say, as I pour this liquid on my father's tomb.°
Shall I say this sentence, regular in human use:
"Grant good return to those who send to you these flowers
of honor: gifts to match the—evil they have done."   95
Or, quiet and dishonored, as my father died
shall I pour out this offering for the ground to drink,
and go, like one who empties garbage out of doors,
and turn my eyes, and throw the vessel far away?
Dear friends, in this deliberation stay with me.   100
We hold a common hatred in this house. Do not
for fear of any, hide your thought inside your heart.
The day of destiny waits for the free man as well
as for the man enslaved beneath an alien hand.
If you know any better course than mine, tell me.   105

CHORUS LEADER
In reverence for your father's tomb as if it were
an altar, I will speak my heart's thought, as you ask.

ELECTRA
Tell me then, please, as you respect my father's grave.

CHORUS LEADER
Say words of grace for those of goodwill, as you pour.

ELECTRA
Whom of those closest to me can I call my friend?   110

CHORUS LEADER
Yourself first; all who hate Aegisthus after that.

ELECTRA
You mean these prayers shall be for you, and for myself?

CHORUS LEADER
You see it now; but it is you whose thought this is.

ELECTRA
Is there some other we should bring in on our side?

CHORUS LEADER
Remember Orestes, though he wanders far away.   115

ELECTRA
That was well spoken; you did well reminding me.

CHORUS LEADER
Remember, too, the murderers, and against them . . .

ELECTRA
What shall I say? Guide and instruct my ignorance.

CHORUS LEADER
Invoke the coming of some man, or more than man.

ELECTRA
To come to judge them, or to give them punishment?   120

CHORUS LEADER

Say simply: "one to kill them, for the life they took."

ELECTRA

I can ask this, and not be wrong in the gods' eyes?

CHORUS LEADER

Of course, to hurt your enemy when he struck first.

ELECTRA

Almighty herald of the world above, the world
below:° Hermes, lord of the dead, help me; announce
my prayers to the charmed spirits underground, who watch   125
over my father's house, that they may hear. Tell Earth
herself, who brings all things to birth, who gives them
    strength,
then gathers their big yield into herself at last.
I myself pour these lustral waters to the dead,
and speak, and call upon my father: Pity me;   130
pity your own Orestes. How shall we be lords
in our house? We have been sold, and go as wanderers
because our mother bought herself, for us, a man,
Aegisthus, he who helped her hand to cut you down.
Now I am what a slave is, and Orestes lives   135
outcast from his great properties, while they go proud
in the high style and luxury of what you worked
to win. By some good fortune let Orestes come
back home. Such is my prayer, my father. Hear me; hear.
And for myself, grant that I be more temperate   140
of heart than my mother; that I act with purer hand.
Such are my prayers for us; but for our enemies,
father, I pray that your avenger come, that they
who killed you shall be killed in turn, as they deserve.
Between my prayer for good and prayer for good I set   145
this prayer for evil; and I speak it against Them.
For us, bring blessings up into the world. Let Earth
and conquering Justice, and all gods beside, give aid.

Such are my prayers; and over them I pour these drink
offerings.

(To the Chorus.)

Yours the mode now, yours to make these flower   150
with fierce laments, and incantation for the dead.

CHORUS [*singing*]
Let the tear fall, that clashes as it dies
as died our fallen lord;
die on this mound that fences good from evil,
washing away the death stain accursed   155
of drink offerings shed. Hear me, oh hear, my lord,
majesty hear me from your dark heart; oh hear,
oh oh!
Let one come, in strength
of spear, some man at arms who will set free the house   160
holding the Scythian bow backbent in his hands,
a mighty god of war spattering arrows
or closing to combat, with sword hilted fast to his hand.

ELECTRA
Father, the earth has drunk my offerings poured to you.   165
But something has happened here, my women. Help me now.

CHORUS LEADER
Speak, if you will. My heart is in a dance of fear.

ELECTRA
Someone has cut a strand of hair and laid it on
the tomb.

CHORUS LEADER
What man? Or was it some slim-waisted girl?

ELECTRA
There is a mark, which makes it plain for any to guess.   170

CHORUS LEADER
Explain, and let your youth instruct my greater age.

ELECTRA

No one could have cut off this strand, except myself.

CHORUS LEADER

Those others, for whom it were proper, are full of hate.

ELECTRA

Yet here it is, and for appearance matches well . . .

CHORUS LEADER

With whose hair? Tell me. This is what I long to know . . .   175

ELECTRA

With my own hair. It is almost exactly like.

CHORUS LEADER

Can it then be a secret gift from Orestes?

ELECTRA

It seems that it must be nobody's hair but his.

CHORUS LEADER

Did Orestes dare to come back here? How could this be?

ELECTRA

He sent it, this severed strand, to do my father honor.   180

CHORUS LEADER

It will not stop my tears if you are right. You mean
that he can never again set foot upon this land.

ELECTRA

The bitter wash has surged upon my heart as well.
I am struck through, as by the cross-stab of a sword,
and from my eyes the thirsty and unguarded drops   185
burst in a storm of tears like winter rain, as I
look on this strand of hair. How could I think some other
man, one of the citizens, could ever be lord of hair like this?
She never could have cut it, she who murdered him
and is my mother, but no mother in her heart   190
which has assumed god's hate and hates her children. No.

And yet, how can I say in open outright confidence
this is a treasured token from the best beloved
of men to me, Orestes? Does hope fawn on me?
Ah
I wish it had the kind voice of a messenger   195
so that my mind would not be torn in two, I not
shaken, but it could tell me plain to throw this strand°
away as trash, if it was cut from a hated head,
or like a brother could have mourned with me, and been
a treasured splendor for my father, and his grave.   200
     The gods know, and we call upon the gods; they know
how we are spun in circles like seafarers, in
what storms. But if we are to win, and our ship live,
from one small seed could burgeon an enormous tree.
But see, here is another sign. Footprints are here.   205
The feet that made them are alike, and look like mine.
There are two sets of footprints: of the man who gave
his hair, and one who shared the road with him. I step
where he has stepped, and heelmarks, and the space between
his heel and toe are like the prints I make. Oh, this   210
is torment, and my wits are going.

(Orestes comes forward from his place of concealment.)

ORESTES

Pray for what is to come, and tell the gods that they
have brought your former prayers to pass. Pray for success.

ELECTRA

Upon what ground? What have I won yet from the gods?

ORESTES

You have come in sight of all you long since prayed to see. 215

ELECTRA

How do you know what man was subject of my prayer?

ORESTES

I know about Orestes, how he stirred your heart.

ELECTRA

Yes; but how am I given an answer to my prayers?

ORESTES

Look at me. Look for no one closer to you than I.

ELECTRA

Is this some net of treachery you catch me in, stranger?   220

ORESTES

Then I must be contriving plots against myself.

ELECTRA

It is your pleasure to laugh at my unhappiness.

ORESTES

I only mock my own then, if I laugh at you.

ELECTRA

Are you really Orestes? Can I call you by that name?

ORESTES

You see my actual self and are slow to learn. And yet   225
you saw this strand of hair I cut in sign of grief
and shuddered with excitement, for you thought you saw
me, and again when you were measuring my tracks.
Now lay the severed strand against where it was cut
and see how well your brother's hair matches my head.°   230
Look at this piece of weaving, the work of your hand
with its blade strokes and figured design of beasts. No, no,
control yourself, and do not lose your head for joy.
I know those nearest to us hate us bitterly.

ELECTRA

O dearest, treasured darling of my father's house,   235
hope of the seed of our salvation, wept for, trust
your strength of hand, and win your father's house again.
O bright beloved presence, you bring back four lives
to me. To call you father is constraint of fact,
and all the love I could have borne my mother turns   240
your way, while she is loathed as she deserves; my love

for a pitilessly slaughtered sister turns to you.
And now you were my steadfast brother after all.
You alone bring me honor; but may Force, and Right,
and Zeus almighty, third with them, be on your side.°   245

ORESTES

Zeus, Zeus, gaze on all that we try to do. Behold
the orphaned children of the eagle-father, now
that he has died entangled in the twisting coils
of the deadly viper, and the young he left behind
are worn with the wasting of starvation, not full grown   250
to bring home to their nest the prey as their father did.
I, with my sister, whom I name, Electra here,
stand in your sight, children whose father is lost. We both
are driven in exile from the house that should be ours.
If you destroy these father's fledglings who gave you°   255
sacrifice and high honor, from what hand like his
shall you be given the sacred feast which is your right?
Destroy the eagle's brood, and you have no more means
to send your signs to mortals for their strong belief;
nor, if the stump rot through on this our royal tree,   260
shall it sustain your altars on sacrificial days.
Safe keep it: from a little thing you can raise up
a house to grandeur, though it now seem overthrown.

CHORUS

O children, silence! Saviors of your father's house,
be silent, children. Otherwise someone may hear   265
and for mere love of gossip carry news of all
you do, to those in power, to those I long to see
some day as corpses in the bubbling pitch and flame.

ORESTES

The big strength of Apollo's oracle will not
forsake me. For he charged me to win through this hazard,   270
with divination of much, and speech articulate,
warning of chill disaster under my warm heart
were I to fail against my father's murderers;

told me to cut them down in their own fashion, turn
to bull-like fury in the loss of my estates.   275
He said that else I must myself pay penalty
with my own life, and suffer much grim punishment;
spoke of the angers that come out of the ground from those
beneath who turn against men; spoke of sicknesses,
ulcers that ride upon the flesh, and cling, and with   280
wild teeth eat away the natural tissue, how on this
disease shall grow in turn a leprous fur. He spoke
of other ways again by which the Avengers might
attack, brought to fulfillment from my father's blood.
There's a dark weapon of those dead men underground   285
all those within my family who fell turn to call
upon me; madness and empty terror in the night
on one who sees clear those visions in the dark:
they tear him loose and shake him until, with all his body
degraded by the collar of bronze, he flees his city.°   290
And such as he can have no share in the communal bowl
allowed them, no cup filled for friends to drink. The wrath
of the father comes unseen on them to drive them back
from altars. None can take them in nor shelter them.
Dishonored and unloved by all the man must die   295
at last, shrunken and wasted away in painful death.
      Shall I not trust such oracles as this? Even if
I do not trust them, here is work that must be done.
Here numerous desires converge to drive me on:
the god's urgency and grief for my father, and with these   300
the loss of my estates wears hard on me; also
the thought that these my citizens, most high renowned
of men, who toppled Troy with hearts of valor, must
go subject to this pair of women; since "his" heart
is really female; or, if not, that soon will show.   305

CHORUS [chanting]
   Almighty Destinies, by the will
   of Zeus let these things

be done, in the turning of Justice.
In return for the word of hatred spoken, let hate
be a word fulfilled. The spirit of Right   310
cries out aloud and extracts atonement
due: blood stroke for the stroke of blood
shall be paid. Who acts, shall suffer. So speaks
the voice of the age-old wisdom.

ORESTES° [singing throughout this lyric interchange with Electra and
the Chorus]

STROPHE A

Father, O my dread father, what thing   315
can I say, can I accomplish
from this far place where I stand, to mark
and reach you there in your chamber
with light that will match your dark?
Yet it is called an action   320
of grace to mourn in style for the house,
once great, of the sons of Atreus.

CHORUS [singing]

STROPHE B

Child, when the fire burns
and tears with its teeth at the dead man   325
it cannot wear out the proud spirit.
He shows his wrath in the after-
days. One dies, and is lamented.
Light falls on the man who killed him.
He is hunted down by the deathsong
for sires slain and for fathers,   330
disturbed, and stern, and avenging.

ELECTRA [singing throughout this lyric interchange]

ANTISTROPHE A

Hear me, my father; hear in turn
all the tears of my sorrows.
Two children stand at your tomb to sing

the burden of your death chant.   335
Your grave is shelter to suppliants,
shelter to the outdriven.
What here is good; what escape from grief?
Can we outwrestle disaster?

CHORUS [*chanting*]
Yet from such as this the god, if he will,   340
can work out strains that are fairer.
For dirges chanted over the grave,
the winner's song in the royal house;
bring home to new arms the beloved.

ORESTES

STROPHE C

If only at Ilium,   345
father, and by some Lycian's hands
you had gone down at the spear's stroke,
you would have left high fame in your house,
for your children seen in the streets
admiration from all;   350
your tomb would be a deep piled bank of earth
founded in a land across the sea,
a light burden for your household;

CHORUS [*singing*]

ANTISTROPHE B

loved then by those he loved
down there beneath the ground   355
who died as heroes, he would have held
state, and a lord's majesty,
vassal only to those most great,
the kings of the underdarkness.
For he was king on earth when he lived°   360
over those whose hands held power of life
and death, and the staff of authority.

ELECTRA

No, but not under Troy's
ramparts, father, should you have died,
nor, with the rest of the spearstruck hordes   365
have found your grave by Scamandrus' crossing.
Sooner, his murderers
should have been killed, as he was,
by those they loved, and have found their death,
and people remote from this outrage   370
had heard the distant story.

CHORUS [chanting]

Child, child, you are dreaming, and dreaming is a light
pastime, of fortune more golden than gold
or the Blessed Ones north of the North Wind.
But the stroke of the twofold lash is pounding   375
close. Helpers are gathering underground
for some of us, while the hands of those who rule
are unclean, and these are accursed.
Power grows on the side of the children.°

ORESTES

This cry has come to my ear   380
like a deep-driven arrow.
Zeus, Zeus, send up from below
ground the delayed destruction
on the cruel heart and the all-daring
hand, for the right of our fathers.   385

CHORUS [singing]

May I claim the right to close the deathsong°
chanted in glory across
the man speared and the woman
dying. Why hide what deep within my breast always   390

flitters? Long since against the heart's
stem a bitter wind has blown
fierce anger and burdened hatred.

ELECTRA

ANTISTROPHE D

May Zeus, from all shoulder's strength,
pound down his fist upon them,   395
ah, ah! smash their heads.
Let the land once more believe.
There has been wrong done. I ask for right.
Hear me, Earth. Hear me, grandeurs of Darkness.

CHORUS [chanting]

It is but law that when the red drops have been spilled   400
upon the ground they cry aloud for fresh
blood. For the death act calls out on Fury
to bring up from those who were slain before
new ruin on ruin accomplished.

ORESTES

STROPHE F

Hear me, you lordships of the world below.   405
Behold in assembled power, curses come from the dead,
behold the last of the sons of Atreus, foundering
lost, without future, cast
from house and right. O Zeus, where shall we turn?

CHORUS [singing throughout the rest of this lyric interchange]

ANTISTROPHE E

The heart jumps in me once again   410
to hear this piteous prayer.
Disconsolate then was I
and now my heart darkens within
deep down, to hear you speak it.   415
But when strength came back hope lifted
me again, and the sorrow
was gone and the light was on me.°

ELECTRA

Of what thing can we speak, and strike more close,
than of the sorrows they who bore us have given?
So let her fawn if she likes. It softens not.   420
For we are bloody like the wolf
and savage born from the savage mother.

CHORUS

I struck my breast in the stroke-style of the Arian,
the Cissian mourning woman,
and the hail-beat of the drifting fists was there to see   425
as the rising pace went in a pattern of blows
downward and upward until the crashing strokes
played on my hammered, my all-stricken head.

ELECTRA

O cruel, cruel
all-daring mother, in cruel processional   430
with all his citizens gone,
with all sorrow for him forgotten
you dared bury your unbewept lord.

ORESTES

O all unworthy of him, what you tell me.
Shall she not pay for this dishonor   435
for all the immortals,
for all my own hands can do?
Let me but take her life and die for it.

CHORUS

Know then, they hobbled him beneath the armpits,
with his own hands. She wrought so, in his burial   440
to make his death a burden

beyond your strength to carry.
The mutilation of your father. Hear it.

ELECTRA

ANTISTROPHE G

You tell of how my father was murdered. Meanwhile I
stood apart, dishonored, nothing worth,   445
in the dark corner, as you would kennel a vicious dog,
and burst in an outrush of tears, that came that day
where smiles would not, and hid the streaming of my grief.
Hear such, and carve the letters of it on your heart.   450

CHORUS

ANTISTROPHE H

Let words such as these
drip deep in your ears, but on a quiet heart.
So far all stands as it stands;
what is to come, yourself burn to know.
You must be hard, give no ground, to win home.   455

ORESTES

STROPHE K

I speak to you. Be with those you love, my father.

ELECTRA

And I, all in my tears, ask with him.

CHORUS

We gather into murmurous revolt. Hear
us, hear. Come back into the light.
Be with us against those we hate.   460

ORESTES

ANTISTROPHE K

War-strength shall collide with war-strength; right with right.

ELECTRA

O gods, be just in what you bring to pass.

CHORUS
    My flesh crawls as I listen to them pray.
    The day of doom has waited long.
    They call for it. It may come.   465

            STROPHE L

O pain grown into the race
and blood-dripping stroke
and grinding cry of disaster,
moaning and impossible weight to bear.
Sickness that fights all remedy.   470

          ANTISTROPHE L

Here in the house resides
the cure for this, not to be brought
from outside, never from others
but within themselves, through the raw brutal bloodshed.
Here is the song sung to the gods beneath us.   475

[*chanting*]
Hear then, you blessed ones under the ground,
and answer these prayers with strength on our side,
free gift for your children's conquest.

ORESTES [*now speaking*]
    Father, O King who died no kingly death, I ask
    the gift of lordship at your hands, to rule your house.   480

ELECTRA [*speaking*]
    I too, my father, ask of you such grace as this:
    to murder Aegisthus with strong hand, and then go free.°

ORESTES
    So shall your memory have the feasts that men honor
    in custom. Otherwise at the tables when offerings
    burn for the earth, you shall be there, but none give heed.   485

ELECTRA
    I too out of my own full dowry then shall bring

libations for my bridal from my father's house.
Of all tombs, yours shall be the lordliest in my eyes.

ORESTES

O Earth, let my father emerge to watch me fight.

ELECTRA

Persephone, grant still the wonder of success. 490

ORESTES

Think of that bath, father, where you were stripped of life.

ELECTRA

Think of the casting net that they contrived for you.

ORESTES

They caught you like a beast in toils no bronzesmith made.

ELECTRA

Rather, hid you in shrouds that were thought out in shame.

ORESTES

Will you not waken, father, to these reproaches? 495

ELECTRA

Will you not raise upright that best beloved head?

ORESTES

Send out your Right to battle on the side of those
you love, or give us holds like those they caught you in.
For they threw you. Would you not see them thrown in turn?

ELECTRA

Hear one more cry, father, from me. It is my last. 500
Your nestlings huddle suppliant at your tomb: look forth
and pity them, female with the male strain alike.

ORESTES°

Do not wipe out this seed of the Pelopidae.
So, though you died, you shall not yet be dead, for when
a man dies, children are the voice of his salvation 505

afterward. Like corks upon the net, these hold
the drenched and flaxen meshes, and they will not drown.
Hear us, then. Our complaints are for your sake, and if
you honor this our argument, you save yourself.

CHORUS LEADER

None can find fault with the length of this discourse you drew   510
out, to show honor to a grave and fate unwept
before. The rest is action. Since your heart is set
that way, now you must strike and prove your destiny.

ORESTES

So. But I am not wandering from my strict course
when I ask why she sent these libations, for what cause   515
she acknowledges, too late, a crime for which there is
no cure. Here was a wretched grace brought to a man°
dead and unfeeling. This I fail to understand.
The offerings are too small for the act done. Pour out
all your possessions to atone one act of blood,   520
you waste your work, it is all useless, reason says.
Explain me this, for I would learn it, if you know.

CHORUS LEADER

I know, child, I was there. It was the dreams she had.
The godless woman had been shaken in the night
by floating terrors, when she sent these offerings.   525

ORESTES

Do you know the dream, too? Can you tell it to me right?

CHORUS LEADER

She told me herself. She dreamed she gave birth to a snake.

ORESTES

What is the end of the story then? What is the point?

CHORUS LEADER

She wrapped it warm in clothing as if it were a child.

ORESTES

A little monster. Did it want some kind of food?   530

CHORUS LEADER

She herself, in the dream, gave it her breast to suck.

ORESTES

How was her nipple not torn by such a beastly thing?

CHORUS LEADER

It was. The creature drew in blood along with the milk.

ORESTES

No vapid dream this. A man is the vision's subject.°

CHORUS LEADER

She woke screaming out of her sleep, shaky with fear,   535
as torches were kindled all about the house, out of
the blind dark that had been on them, to comfort the queen.
So now she sends these mourning offerings to be poured
and hopes they are medicinal for her disease.

ORESTES

But I pray to the earth and to my father's grave   540
that this dream is for me and that I will succeed.
See, I divine it, and it coheres all in one piece.
If this snake came out of the same place whence I came,
if she wrapped it in robes, as she wrapped me, and if
its jaws gaped wide around the breast that suckled me,   545
and if it stained the intimate milk with an outburst
of blood, so that for fright and pain she cried aloud,
it follows then, that as she nursed this hideous thing
of prophecy, she must be cruelly murdered. I
turn snake to kill her. This is what the dream speaks loud.   550

CHORUS LEADER

I choose you my interpreter to read these dreams.
So may it happen. Now you must rehearse your side
in their parts. For some, this means the parts they must not
    play.

ORESTES

Simple to tell them. My sister here must go inside.

I charge her to keep secret what we have agreed, 555
so that, as they by treachery killed a man of high
degree, by treachery tangled in the self-same net
they too shall die, in the way Loxias has ordained,
my lord Apollo, whose word was never false before.
Disguised as an outlander, for which I have all gear, 560
I shall go to the outer gates with Pylades
whom you see here. He is hereditary friend
and companion-in-arms of my house. We two shall both
     assume
the Parnassian dialect and imitate the way
they talk in Phocis. If none at the door will take us in 565
kindly, because the house is in a curse of ills,
we shall stay there, till anybody who goes by
the house will wonder why we are shut out, and say:
"Why does Aegisthus keep the suppliant turned away
from his gates, if he is hereabouts and knows of this?" 570
But if I once cross the doorstone of the outer gates
and find my man seated upon my father's throne,
or if he comes down to confront me, and uplifts
his eyes to mine, then lets them drop again, be sure,
before he can say: "Where does the stranger come from?" I 575
shall plunge my sword with lightning speed, and drop him
     dead.
Our Fury who is never starved for blood shall drink
for the third time a cupful of unwatered blood.
     Electra, keep a careful eye on all within
the house, so that our plans will hold together.

                                        (To the Chorus.)

                              You, 580
women: I charge you, hold your tongues religiously.
Be silent if you must, or speak in the way that will
help us. And now I call upon the god who stands
close, to look on, and guide the actions of my sword.

(Exit Orestes and Pylades to the side, Electra into the palace.)

CHORUS [*singing*]

STROPHE A

Numberless, the earth breeds   585
dangers, and the awful thought of fear.
The bending sea's arms swarm
with bitter, savage beasts.
Torches blossom to burn along
the high space between ground and sky.   590
Things fly, and things walk the earth.
Remember too
the storm and wrath of the whirlwind.

ANTISTROPHE A

But who can recount all
the high daring in the will   595
of man, and in the stubborn hearts of women
the all-adventurous passions
that couple with man's overthrow.
The female force, the desperate
love crams its resisted way
on marriage and the dark embrace   600
of brute beasts, of mortal men.

STROPHE B

Let him, who goes not on flimsy wings
of thought, learn from her.
Althaea, Thestius'   605
daughter: who maimed her child, and hard
of heart, in deliberate guile
set fire to the bloody torch, her own son's
age-mate, that from the day he emerged
from the mother's womb crying   610
shared the measure of all his life
down to the marked death day.

ANTISTROPHE B

And in the legends there is one more, a girl
of blood, figure of hate
who, for the enemy's
sake killed one near in blood, seduced by the wrought   615
golden necklace from Crete,
wherewith Minos bribed her. She sundered
from Nisus his immortal hair   620
as he all unsuspecting
breathed in a tranquil sleep. Foul wretch,
Hermes of death has got her now.

STROPHE C

Since I recall cruelties from quarrels long
ago, in vain, and married love turned to bitterness
a house would fend far away   625
by curse; the guile, treacheries of the woman's heart
against a lord armored in
power, a lord his enemies revered,°
I prize the hearth not inflamed within the house,
the woman's right pushed not into daring.   630

ANTISTROPHE C

Of all foul things told in legend the Lemnian
outranks, a vile wizard's charm, detestable
so that men name a hideous
crime "Lemnian" in memory of that wickedness.
When once the gods loathe a breed   635
of men they go outcast and forgotten.
No man respects what the gods have turned against.
What of these tales I gather has no meaning?

STROPHE D

The sword edges near the lungs.
It stabs deep, bittersharp,   640
and Right drives it. For that which had no right

lies not yet stamped into the ground, although
one in sin transgressed Zeus' majesty.   645

Right's anvil stands staunch on the ground
and the smith, Destiny, hammers out the sword.
Delayed in glory, pensive from
the murk, Vengeance brings home at last   650
a child, to wipe out the stain of blood shed long ago.

*(Enter Orestes and Pylades from the side, carrying
baggage and dressed as travelers.)*

ORESTES

In there! Inside! Does anyone hear me knocking at
the gate? I will try again. Is anyone at home?
Try a third time. I ask for someone to come from the house,   655
if Aegisthus lets it welcome friendly visitors.

SERVANT   *(Inside.)*

All right, I hear you. Where does the stranger come from,
then?

ORESTES

Announce me to the masters of the house. It is
to them I come, and I have news for them to hear.
And be quick, for the darkening chariot of night   660
leans to its course; the hour for wayfarers to drop
anchor in some place that entertains all travelers.
Have someone of authority in the house come out,
the lady of the place or, more appropriately,
its lord, for then no delicacy in speaking blurs   665
the spoken word. A man takes courage and speaks out
to another man, and makes clear everything he means.

(Enter Clytaemestra from inside the palace.)

CLYTAEMESTRA

Friends, tell me only what you would have, and it is yours.
We have all comforts that go with a house like ours,

hot baths, and beds to charm away your weariness   670
with rest, and the regard of honest eyes. But if
you have some higher business, more a matter of state,
that is the men's concern, and I will tell them of it.

ORESTES

I am a Daulian stranger out of Phocis. As
I traveled with my pack and my own following   675
making for Argos, where my feet are rested now,
I met a man I did not know, nor did he know
me, but he asked what way I took, and told me his.
It was a Phocian, Strophius; for he told me his name
and said: "Friend, since in any case you make for Argos,   680
remember carefully to tell Orestes' parents
that he is dead; please do not let it slip your mind.
Then, if his people decide to have him brought back home,
or bury him where he went to live, all outlander   685
forever, carry their requests again to me.
For as it is, the bronze walls of an urn close in
the ashes of a man who has been deeply mourned."
So much I know, no more. But whether I now talk
with those who have authority and concern in this
I do not know. I think his father should be told.   690

CLYTAEMESTRA

Ah me. You tell us how we are stormed from head to heel.
Oh curse upon our house, bitter antagonist,
how far your eyes range. What was clean out of your way
your archery brings down with a distant deadly shot
to strip unhappy me of all I ever loved.   695
Even Orestes now! He was so well advised
to keep his foot clear of this swamp of death. But now
set down as traitor the hope that was our healer once
and made us look for a bright revel in our house.

ORESTES

I could have wished, with hosts so prosperous as you,   700
to have made myself known by some more gracious news

and so been entertained by you. For what is there
more kindly than the feeling between host and guest?
Yet it had been abuse of duty in my heart
had I not given so great a matter to his friends,   705
being so bound by promise and the stranger's rights.

CLYTAEMESTRA

You shall not find that your reception falls below
your worth, nor be any the less our friend for this.
Some other would have brought the news in any case.
But it is the hour for travelers who all day have trudged   710
the long road, to be given the rest that they deserve.
Escort this gentleman with his companion and
his men, to where our male friends are made at home.
Look after them, in manner worthy of a house
like ours; you are responsible for their good care.   715
Meanwhile, we shall communicate these matters to
the masters of the house, and with our numerous friends
deliberate the issues of this fatal news.

(Exit all but the Chorus, into the palace.)

CHORUS [*chanting*]

Handmaidens of this house, who help our cause,
how can our lips frame   720
some force that will show for Orestes?
    O Lady Earth, Earth Queen, who now
ride mounded over the lord of ships
where the king's corpse lies buried,
hear us, help us.   725
Now the time breaks for Persuasion in stealth
to go down to the Pit, with Hermes of death°
and the dark, to direct
trial by the sword's fierce edge.

CHORUS LEADER

I think our newcomer is at his deadly work;   730
I see Orestes' old nurse coming forth, in tears.

(Enter the Nurse, Cilissa, from inside the palace.)

Now where are you going, Cilissa, through the palace gates,
with sorrow as your hireless fellow wayfarer?

NURSE

The woman who is our mistress told me to make haste
and summon Aegisthus for the strangers, "so that he   735
can come and hear, as man to man, in more detail
this news that they have brought." She put a sad face on
before the servants, to hide the smile inside her eyes
over this work that has been done so happily
for her—though on this house the misery is now complete   740
from the plain story that the stranger men have brought.
But as for that Aegisthus, oh, he will be pleased
enough to hear the story. Poor unhappy me,
all my long-standing mixture of misfortunes, hard
burden enough, here in this house of Atreus,   745
when it befell me made the heart ache in my breast.
But never yet did I have to bear a hurt like this.
I took the other troubles bravely as they came:
but now, darling Orestes! I wore out my life
for him. I took him from his mother, brought him up.   750
There were times when he screamed at night and woke me
    from
my rest; I had to do many hard tasks, and now
useless; a baby is like a beast, it does not think
but you have to nurse it, do you not, the way it wants.
For the child still in swaddling clothes cannot tell us   755
if he is hungry or thirsty, if he needs to make
water. Children's young insides are a law to themselves.
I needed second sight for this, and many a time
I think I missed, and had to wash the baby's clothes.
The nurse and laundrywoman had a combined duty   760
and that was I. I was skilled in both handicrafts,
and so Orestes' father gave him to my charge.
And now, unhappy, I am told that he is dead

and go to take the story to that man who has
defiled our house; he will be glad to hear such news.   765

CHORUS LEADER

Did she say he should come back armed in any way?

NURSE

How, armed? Say it again. I do not understand.

CHORUS LEADER

Was he to come with bodyguards, or by himself?

NURSE

She said to bring his followers, the men-at-arms.

CHORUS LEADER

Now, if you hate our master, do not tell him that,   770
but simply bid him come as quickly as he can
and cheerfully. In that way he will not take fright.
It is the messenger who makes the bent word straight.

NURSE

But are you happy over what I have told you?

CHORUS LEADER

Perhaps: if Zeus might turn our evil wind to good.   775

NURSE

How so? Orestes, once hope of the house, is gone.

CHORUS LEADER

Not yet. It would be a poor seer who saw it thus.

NURSE

What is this? Have you some news that has not been told?

CHORUS LEADER

Go on and take your message, do as you were bid.
The gods' concerns are what concern only the gods.   780

NURSE

I will go then and do all this as you have told
me to. May all be for the best. So grant us god.

CHORUS [*singing*]

STROPHE A

Now to my supplication. Zeus,
father of Olympian gods,
grant that those who struggle hard to see   785
temperate things done in the house win their aim°
in full. All that I spoke
was spoken in right. Yours, Zeus, to protect.

MESODE

Zeus, Zeus, make him who is now
in the house stand above those who
hate. If you rear him to greatness,   790
double and three times
and blithely he will repay you.

ANTISTROPHE A

See the colt of this man whom you loved
harnessed to the chariot   795
of suffering. Set upon the race he runs
sure control. Make us not see him break
stride, but clean down the course
keep the pace of his striding speed.

STROPHE B

You that, deep in the house   800
sway their secret pride of wealth,
hear us, gods of sympathy.
For things done in time past°
wash out the blood in fair-spoken verdict.   805
Let the old murder in
the house breed no more.

MESODE

And you, who keep, magnificent, the hallowed and huge
cavern, O grant that the man's house lift up its head

and look on the shining of daylight
and liberty with eyes made 810
glad with gazing out from the helm of darkness.

ANTISTROPHE B

And with Right may the son
of Maia lend his hand, strong to send
wind fair for action, if he will.
Much else lies secret he may show at need. 815
He speaks the secret word, by
night hoods darkness on the eyes
nor shows more plainly when the day is there.

STROPHE C

Then at last we shall sing
for deliverance of the house 820
the woman's song that sets the wind
fair, no thin-drawn and grief-
struck wail, but this: "The ship sails fair."
My way, mine, the advantage piles here, with wreck 825
and ruin far from those I love.

MESODE

Be not fear-struck when your turn comes in the action,
but with a great cry "Father"
when she cries "Child" to you
go on through with the innocent murder. 830

ANTISTROPHE C

Yours to raise high within
your body the heart of Perseus
and for those under the ground you loved
and those yet above, to exact
what their bitter passion may desire; make 835
bloody ruin of the Gorgon inside the house;°
wipe out the man stained with murder.

(Enter Aegisthus from the side, alone.)

AEGISTHUS

It is not without summons that I come, but called
by messenger, with news that there are strangers here
arrived, telling a story that brings no delight: 840
the death of Orestes. For our house, already bitten
and poisoned, to take this new load upon itself
would be a thing of dripping fear and blood. Yet how
shall I pass upon these rumors? As the living truth?
For messages made out of women's terror leap   845
high in the upward air and empty die. Do you
know anything of this by which to clear my mind?

CHORUS LEADER

We heard, yes. But go on inside and hear it from
the strangers. Messengers are never quite so sure
as a man's questions answered by the men themselves.   850

AEGISTHUS

I wish to question, carefully, this messenger
and learn if he himself was by when the man died
or if he heard but some blind rumor and so speaks.
The mind has eyes, not to be easily deceived.

(Aegisthus goes inside.)

CHORUS [*chanting*]

Zeus, Zeus, what shall I say, where make   855
a beginning of prayer for the gods' aid?
My will is good
but how shall I speak to match my need?
The bloody edges of the knives that rip   860
man-flesh are moving to work. It will mean
utter and final ruin imposed
on Agamemnon's
house, or our man will kindle a flame
and light of liberty, win the domain
and huge treasure again of his fathers.   865
Forlorn challenger, though blessed by god,

Orestes must come to grips with two,
so wrestle. Yet may he throw them.

(A shriek is heard from inside the house.)

[*singing*]
Listen, it goes   870
but how? What has been done in the house?

CHORUS LEADER [*speaking*]
    Stand we aside until the work is done, for so
we shall not seem to be accountable in this
foul business. For the fight is done, the issue drawn.

(Enter a Follower of Aegisthus, running from inside the house.)

FOLLOWER
    O sorrow, all is sorrow for our stricken lord.   875
Raise up again a triple cry of sorrow, for
Aegisthus lives no longer. Open there, open
quick as you may, and slide back the door bars on the
    women's
gates. It will take the strength of a young arm, but not
to fight for one who is dead and done for. What use there?   880
Ho there, ho!
My cry is to the deaf and I babble in vain
at sleepers to no purpose. Clytaemestra, where
is she, does what? Her neck is on the razor's edge
and ripe for lopping, as she did to others before.

(Enter Clytaemestra.)

CLYTAEMESTRA
    What is this, and why are you shouting in the house?   885

FOLLOWER
    I tell you, the living are being killed by the dead ones.

CLYTAEMESTRA
    Ah, so. You speak in riddles, but I read the rhyme.

We have been won with the treachery by which we slew.
Bring me quick, somebody, an axe to kill a man

(Exit Follower.)

and we shall see if we can beat him before we   890
go down—so far gone are we in this wretched fight.

(Enter Orestes and Pylades from the palace, with swords drawn.)

ORESTES
You next: the other one in there has had enough.

CLYTAEMESTRA
Beloved, strong Aegisthus, are you dead indeed?

ORESTES
You love your man, then? You shall lie in the same grave
with him, and never be unfaithful even in death.   895

CLYTAEMESTRA
Hold, my son. Oh take pity, child, before this breast
where many a time, a drowsing baby, you would feed
and with soft gums sucked in the milk that made you strong.

ORESTES
What shall I do, Pylades? Be shamed to kill my mother?

PYLADES
What then becomes thereafter of the oracles   900
declared by Loxias at Pytho? What of sworn oaths?
Count all men hateful to you rather than the gods.

ORESTES
I judge that you win. Your advice is good.

(To Clytaemestra.)

Come here.

My purpose is to kill you over his body.
You thought him bigger than my father while he lived.   905
Die then and sleep beside him, since he is the man
you love, and he you should have loved got only your hate.

CLYTAEMESTRA

I raised you when you were little. May I grow old with you?

ORESTES

You killed my father. Would you make your home with me?

CLYTAEMESTRA

Destiny had some part in that, my child.   910

ORESTES

                                                      Why then
destiny has worked this death for you as well.

CLYTAEMESTRA

A mother has her curse, child. Are you not afraid?

ORESTES

No. You bore me and threw me away, to a hard life.

CLYTAEMESTRA

I sent you to a friend's house. This was no throwing away.

ORESTES

I was born of a free father. You sold me.   915

CLYTAEMESTRA

So? Where then is the price that I received for you?

ORESTES

I could say. It would be indecent to tell you.

CLYTAEMESTRA

Or if you do, tell also your father's follies.

ORESTES

Blame him not. He suffered while you were sitting here at
    home.

CLYTAEMESTRA

It hurts women to be kept from their men, my child.   920

ORESTES

The man's hard work supports the women who sit at home.

CLYTAEMESTRA

I think, child, that you mean to kill your mother.

ORESTES

No.
It will be you who kill yourself. It will not be I.

CLYTAEMESTRA

Take care. Your mother's curse, like dogs, will drag you down.

ORESTES

How shall I escape my father's curse, if I fail here?   925

CLYTAEMESTRA

I feel like one who wastes live tears upon a tomb.

ORESTES

Yes, this is death, your wages for my father's fate.

CLYTAEMESTRA

You are the snake I gave birth to, and gave the breast.

ORESTES

Indeed, the terror of those dreams saw things to come
clearly.° You killed, and it was wrong. Now suffer wrong.   930

(Orestes and Pylades take Clytaemestra into the palace.)

CHORUS LEADER

I have sorrow even for this pair in their twofold
downfall. But since Orestes had the hardiness
to end this chain of bloodlettings, here lies our choice,
that the eyes' light in this house shall not utterly die.

CHORUS [singing]

STROPHE A

Justice came at the last to Priam and all his sons   935
and it was heavy and hard,
but into the house of Agamemnon returned
the double lion, the double assault,
and the Pythian-steered exile

drove home to the hilt
vengeance, moving strongly in guidance sent by the god.   940

Raise up the high cry O over our lordships' house
won free of distress, free of its fortunes wasted
by two stained with murder,
free of its mournful luck.   945

He came back; his work lay in the secret attack
and it was stealthy and hard,
but in the fighting his hand was steered by the very daughter
of Zeus: Right we call her,   950
mortals who speak of her and name her well. Her wind
is fury and death visited upon those she hates.

All that Loxias, who on Parnassus holds
the huge, the deep cleft in the ground, shrilled aloud,
by guile that is no guile   955
returns now to assault the wrong done and grown old.
Divinity keeps, we know not how, strength to resist
surrender to the wicked.
The power that holds the sky's majesty wins our worship.   960

Light is here to behold.
The big bit that curbed our house is taken away.
Rise up, you halls, arise; for time grown too long
you lay tumbled along the ground.

Time brings all things to pass. Presently time shall cross   965
the outgates of the house after the stain is driven
entire from the hearth
by ceremonies that wash clean and cast out the furies.
The dice of fortune shall be thrown once more, and lie

prosperous and smiling   970
up at the new indwellers come to live in the house.

> *(The doors of the house open, to show Orestes standing over the*
> *bodies of Clytaemestra and Aegisthus, while attendants display*
> *the net-like garment in which Clytaemestra had entangled*
> *Agamemnon and which she herself displayed after his murder.)*

ORESTES

Behold the twin tyrannies of our land, these two
who killed my father and who sacked my house. For a time
they sat upon their thrones and kept their pride of state,   975
and they are lovers still. So may you judge by what
befell them, for as they were pledged their oath abides.
They swore together death for my unhappy sire
and swore to die together. Now they keep their oath.
Behold again, O audience of these evil things,   980
the engine against my wretched father they devised,
the hands' entanglement, the hobbles for his feet.
Spread it out. Stand around me in a circle and
display this net that caught a man. So shall, not my
father, but that great father who sees all, the Sun,   985
look on my mother's sacrilegious handiwork
and be a witness for me in my day of trial
how it was in all right that I achieved this death,
my mother's: for of Aegisthus' death I take no count:
he has his seducer's punishment, no more than law.   990
But she, who plotted this foul death against the man
by whom she carried the weight of children underneath
her belt, burden once loved, shown hard and hateful now,
what does she seem to be? Some water snake, some viper
whose touch is rot even to him who felt no fang   995
strike, by that brutal and wrong daring in her heart.
And this thing: what shall I call it and be right, in all
eloquence? Trap for an animal or winding sheet
for a dead man? Or bath curtain? Since it is a net,
robe you could call it, to entangle a man's feet.   1000

Some highwayman might own a thing like this, to catch
the wayfarer and rob him of his money and
so make a living. With a treacherous thing like this
he could take many victims and warm his heart within.
May no such partner as she was come to live with me.   1005
Sooner, let god destroy me, with no children born.

CHORUS [*chanting*]
Ah, but the pitiful work.
Dismal the death that was your ending.
He is left alive; pain flowers for him.

ORESTES
Did she do it or did she not? My witness is
this great robe. It was thus she stained Aegisthus' sword.   1010
Dip it and dip it again, the smear of blood conspires
with time to spoil the beauty of this precious thing.
Now I can praise him, now I can stand by to mourn
and speak before this web that killed my father; yet   1015
I grieve for the thing done, the death, and all our race.
I have won; but my victory is polluted, and has no pride.

CHORUS [*chanting*]
There is no mortal man who shall turn
unhurt his life's course to an end not marred.
There is trouble here. There is more to come.   1020

ORESTES
I would have you know, I see not how this thing will end.
I am a charioteer whose course is wrenched outside
the track, for I am beaten, my rebellious senses
bolt with me headlong and the fear against my heart
is ready for the singing and dance of wrath. But while   1025
I hold some grip still on my wits, I say publicly
to my friends: I killed my mother not without some right.
My father's murder stained her, and the gods' disgust.
As for the spells that charmed me to such daring, I   1030
cite above all the seer of Pytho, Loxias. He

declared I could do this and not be charged with wrong,
while if I refused, the punishment I will not speak:
no archery could hit such height of agony.
And look upon me now, how I go armored in
leafed branch and garland on my way to the centerstone   1035
and sanctuary, and Apollo's sacred ground,
the shining of the fabulous fire that never dies,
to escape this blood that is my own. Loxias ordained
that I should turn me to no other shrine than this.
To all men of Argos in time to come I say   1040
they shall be witness, how these evil things were done.
I go, an outcast wanderer from this land, and leave
behind, in life, in death, the name of what I did.

CHORUS LEADER

No, what you did was well done. Do not therefore bind
your mouth to foul speech. Keep no evil on your lips.   1045
You liberated all the Argive city when
you lopped the heads of these two snakes with one clean
    stroke.

ORESTES

No!
Women who serve this house, they come like Gorgons, they
wear robes of black, and they are wreathed in a tangle
of snakes. I can no longer stay.   1050

CHORUS LEADER

Orestes, dearest to your father of all men,
what fancies whirl you? Hold, do not give way to fear.

ORESTES

These are no fancies of affliction. They are clear,
and real, and here; the bloodhounds of my mother's hate.

CHORUS LEADER

It is the blood still wet upon your hands, that makes   1055
this shaken turbulence be thrown upon your sense.

ORESTES

Ah, Lord Apollo, how they grow and multiply,
repulsive for the blood drops of their dripping eyes.

CHORUS LEADER

There is one way to make you clean: let Loxias
touch you, and set you free from these disturbances. 1060

ORESTES

You cannot see them, but I see them. I am driven
from this place. I can stay here no longer.

(*Exit, to the side.*)

CHORUS LEADER

Good luck go with you then, and may the god look on
you with favor and guard you in kind circumstance.

CHORUS [*chanting*]

Here on this house of the kings the third 1065
storm has broken, with wind
from the inward race, and gone its course.
The children were eaten: that was the first
affliction, the curse of Thyestes.
Next came the royal death, when a man 1070
and lord of Achaean armies went down
killed in the bath. Third
is for the savior. He came. Shall I call
it that, or death? Where
is the end? Where shall the fury of fate 1075
be stilled to sleep, be done with?

ELECTRA

SOPHOCLES
Translated by David Grene

INTRODUCTION TO
SOPHOCLES' ELECTRA

There is no external evidence for the date of this play. Most scholars tend to put it late in the career of Sophocles, on stylistic grounds. But there is no certainty.

Sophocles' *Electra* tells the same story as *The Libation Bearers* of Aeschylus and the *Electra* of Euripides. That Sophocles' play is named after the heroine, rather than the hero or chorus, is not without significance. Electra does not disappear halfway through the action, as in Aeschylus; she is the main character. Like Sophocles' *Antigone*, she is given a cautious sister to be a foil to her resolute spirit of resistance; and she is there at the end, spurring her brother on to his murderous work. Another clue to the spirit of the play is found in the instructions of Apollo, quoted by Orestes, near the beginning (lines 37-38):

...take not help of shields nor host; instead,
by myself perform the slaughter, stealthily,
with just but crafty hand.

For "stealthily" we could even read "treacherously." The deception is exploited. Orestes and his old retainer, the Tutor, concoct a story of how Orestes was killed in a racing accident at the Pythian Games; they bring on a funereal urn supposed to contain his ashes. We find, what is contrary to the normal practices of tragedy, a *false* messenger speech; even Electra is deceived.

A final turn is given to the progress of the story by having Clytemnestra killed first. Any incipient feelings of remorse are swallowed in the need for instant action as the approach of Aegisthus is announced, and he is duly eliminated in turn. There are no Furies; there is no flight of Orestes. This is all—and critics are left to come to various conclusions about the morality and characterizations of this play, including the conclusion that there is in the end no conclusion.

ELECTRA

Characters   TUTOR, Orestes' old servant
    ORESTES, son of Agamemnon and Clytemnestra
    PYLADES (silent character), friend of Orestes
    from Phocis
    ELECTRA, daughter of Agamemnon and
    Clytemnestra
    CHORUS of women of Mycenae
    CHRYSOTHEMIS, sister of Electra and Orestes
    CLYTEMNESTRA, widow of Agamemnon and
    wife of Aegisthus
    AEGISTHUS, usurping king of Mycenae

Scene: Before the royal palace in Mycenae.

(Enter Orestes, Pylades, and Tutor, from the side.)

TUTOR

Son of Agamemnon, commander once at Troy,
now you are here, now you can see it all,
all that your heart has always longed for.
This is old Argos of your yearning, the grove
of Inachus' gadfly-haunted daughter, Io.   5
And here, Orestes, is the Lycian marketplace
of the wolf-killing god. Here on the left
the famous temple of Hera. Where we have come now,
believe your eyes, see golden Mycenae,
and here the death-heavy house of the Pelopids.   10

Once on a time, from amidst your father's murder,
I took you from this house, received you from the hand
of your sister, the one who shares your blood.
I saved you then. I have raised you from that day
to this moment of your manhood to be the avenger
of that father done to death. Orestes, now,   15
and you, Pylades, dearest friend, take counsel
quickly on what to do. Already the sunlight,
brightening, stirs dawning birdsong into clearness,
and the black, kindly night of stars is gone.
Before any man leaves the house, you two   20
must join together in discussion. We are where
we must not shrink. It is high time for action.

ORESTES
Dearest of servants:
very plain are the signs you show of your nobility
toward me. It is so with a well-bred horse: 25
even in old age, hard conditions
do not break his spirit. His ears are still erect.
So it is with you. You urge me, and yourself
follow among the first. Therefore, I will make plain
all that I have decided. Give keen ear   30
to what I say, and if I miss the mark
of what I should, correct me.

When I came to Pytho's place of prophecy
to learn how to win revenge
for my father's murder on those that killed him,
Phoebus spoke to me what I tell you now: 35
to take not help of shields nor host; instead,
by myself perform the slaughter, stealthily,
with just but crafty hand.
Now since this was the oracle we heard,
go you into this house when occasion calls you.
Know all that is done there, and, knowing, report   40
clear news to us. You are old. It's a long time.

They won't recognize you. They will not suspect you
with this silver hair of yours. Here is your story.
You are a stranger coming from Phanoteus,   45
their Phocian friend, the greatest of their allies.
Tell them a sudden accident befell
Orestes, and he's dead. Swear it on oath.
Say in the Pythian games he was rolled
out of his chariot at high speed.
Let that be your story.   50

        But we shall go first to my father's grave
and crown it, as the god bade us, with libations
and with luxuriant cuttings from my hair.
And then we shall come back here again
and in our hands a carved bronze-sided urn,
the urn that you know I hid here in the bushes.   55
By these means we shall bring them the pleasant news
with our tale of lies, that my body is no longer,
but has been burned and reduced to ashes.
What harm does it do me if by dying in word
in deed I come through alive and win my glory?   60
To my thinking, no word is bad when spoken with profit.
Before now I have seen wise men often
dying empty deaths as far as words reported them,
and then, when they have come to their homes again,
they have been honored more, even to the skies.
So in my case I venture to predict
that I who die according to this rumor   65
shall, like a blazing star, glare on my foes again.

Land of my father, gods of my country,
welcome me, grant me success in my coming,
and you, too, house of my father;
as your purifier I have come,
in justice sent by the gods.   70
Do not send me dishonored out of this country,
but ancestrally rich, restorer of my house.

This is all that I have to say. Old man,
let it be yours to go and mind your task.
We two must go away. It is the moment,   75
and the moment is greatest master of every act.

ELECTRA [*chanting from inside the house*]
    Ah! Ah! What misery!

TUTOR
    Inside the house I thought I heard someone,
    one of the servants, crying.

ORESTES
                         Might it not be   80
    poor suffering Electra? Would you like us
    to stay here and to listen to her crying?

TUTOR
    No. Nothing must come before our trying
    to carry out what Loxias has bidden us.
    From there we must make our beginning,
    pouring the holy offerings for your father.
    For that, I say, will bring us victory,   85
    and mastery in our enterprise.

                              (*Orestes and the others withdraw to the side.*
                                    Enter Electra from the palace.)

ELECTRA [*chanting*]
    O holy light
    and air, copartner with earth,
    how many songs of lament,
    how many plangent strokes
    beating till my breast was bloody,   90
    have you heard from me
    when the gloomy night has withdrawn?
    And again in the house of my misery
    my bed is witness to my all-night sorrowing
    dirges for my unhappy father.

In the land of the foreigner   95
no murderous god of battles entertained him;
but my mother and the man who shared her bed,
Aegisthus, split his head with a murderous axe,
like woodsmen with an oak tree.
For all this no pity was given you   100
by any but me, no pity for your death,
father, so pitiful, so cruel.
But, for my part, I
will never cease my dirges and sorrowful laments,
as long as I have eyes to see
the ever-shining light of the stars and this daylight.   105
So long, like a nightingale who has lost her young,°
here before the doors of what was my father's house
I shall cry out my sorrow for all the world to hear.

House of Hades, house of Persephone,   110
Hermes of the underworld, mighty Curse,
and Furies, the Dread Ones, children of gods,
who look upon those who die unjustly,
who look upon the marriage bed secretly betrayed,
come all and help take vengeance for my father,   115
for my father's murder!
And send me my brother to my aid.
For alone I am no longer strong enough
to bear the burden of the grief that weighs against me.   120

(Enter the Chorus of Mycenaean women from one side.)

CHORUS [singing]

STROPHE A

Electra, child of the wretchedest of mothers,
why with ceaseless lament do you waste away
sorrowing for one long dead,
Agamemnon, godlessly trapped
by deceits of your treacherous mother,   125
betrayed by her evil hand?

May evil be the end
of the one who contrived the deed,
if it is allowed for me to utter this!

ELECTRA [*also singing*]
Daughters of truehearted families,
you have come to console me in my troubles.   130
I know, I understand what you say,
nothing of it escapes me.
But, all the same, I will not
cease my mourning for my poor father.
You whose love responds to mine in all ways,
allow me thus wildly to grieve,   135
I entreat you.

CHORUS
                    ANTISTROPHE A
But from the all-receptive Lake
of Death you shall not raise him,
groan and pray as you will.
Past the bounds of sense you dwell in grief   140
that is cureless, with sorrow unending,
and you are destroying yourself,
in a matter where the evil knows no deliverance.
Why do you seek
such unbearable suffering?

ELECTRA
Foolish indeed is the one   145
that forgets parents pitifully dead.
Suited rather to my heart
is the bird of mourning
that always laments "Itys, Itys,"
the bird of frenzied sorrow, Zeus's messenger.
And Niobe, that suffered all, ah!   150
I count you as a goddess
as you weep perpetually
in your rocky tomb.

CHORUS

STROPHE B

Not alone to you, my child,
this burden of grief has come: 155
yet you exceed in your feeling far
those of your kin and blood.
Consider Chrysothemis and her life,
and Iphianassa,
and that one who grows up to prosperity in secret,
sorrowing, a prince, 160
whom one day this famed land of Mycenae
shall welcome home as noble heir,
returning here with Zeus' blessing, Orestes.

ELECTRA

I await him always
sadly, unweariedly,
I who am past childbearing,
past marriage, 165
always to my own ruin.
Wet with tears, I endure
an unending doom of misfortune.
But he has forgotten
what he has suffered, what he has known.
What message ever comes from him to me
that does not turn out false? 170
Yes, he is always longing to come,
but he does not choose to come, for all his longing.

CHORUS

ANTISTROPHE B

Take heart, take heart, my child.
Still great above is Zeus,
who oversees all things in sovereign power. 175
Confide to him your overbitter wrath;
do not overburden yourself with hate against
your enemies, nor yet forget them quite:

for Time is a kindly god.
For neither he that lives
by Crisa's cattle-grazing shore, 180
the son of Agamemnon, will be neglectful,
nor the god that rules by Acheron's waters.

ELECTRA

But for me already the most of my life 185
has gone by without hope,
and I have no strength anymore.
I am one wasted in childlessness,
with no loving husband for champion.
Like some dishonored foreigner,
I serve in my father's house in these ugly rags 190
and stand at empty tables.

CHORUS

STROPHE C

Pitiful was the cry at the homecoming,
and pitiful, when on your father on his couch
the sharp biting stroke of the brazen axe
was driven home. 195
Craft was the contriver, lust the killer,
dreadfully begetting between them a shape,
dreadful, whether divine or human,
the one that did this. 200

ELECTRA

That day of all days that have ever been
most deeply hateful to me!
O night, horrible burden
of that unspeakable banquet,
shameful death that my father saw 205
dealt him by the hands of the two,
hands that took my own life captive,
betrayed, destroyed me utterly.
For these deeds may god in his greatness,
the Olympian one, grant punishment to match them, 210

and may they have no profit of glory,
they who accomplished such actions.

CHORUS

ANTISTROPHE C

Take heed you do not speak too far.
Do you not see from what
causes you suffer as you do?
Self-inflicted is the ruin   215
that you've fallen into so wretchedly.
You have won for yourself
superfluity of misfortune,
breeding wars in your sullen soul
evermore. You cannot fight
such conflicts hand to hand, with those who hold power.°   220

ELECTRA

Dreadful things compelled me,
to dreadful things I was driven.
I know it, I know my own spirit.
With dread all around me, I will not hold back
from this wild course of ruin, so long as I live.   225
For who, dear friends, who that thinks right
could expect there to be suitable comforting
words for me?
Let me be, let me be—no more comforting!
These ills of mine shall be called cureless   230
and never shall I cease my sorrow;
the number of my laments will be countless.

CHORUS

EPODE

But only in good will to you I speak
like a loyal mother, entreating you
not to breed ruin from ruin.   235

ELECTRA

What is the natural measure of my sorrow?

Come, how when the dead are in question
can it be honorable to forget?
In what human being is this instinctive?
Never may I have honor among such people,
nor, if I encounter any good thing,   240
may I live at ease with it, by restraining
the wings of shrill lament to my father's dishonor!
For if he that is dead
is earth and nothing,   245
lying in misery,
and they shall never in their turn
pay death for murderous death,
then shall all shame be dead
and all men's piety.   250

CHORUS LEADER [*speaking*]
  My child, it was with both our interests at heart
  I came, both yours and mine. If what I say
  is wrong, have your own way. We will obey you.

ELECTRA [*now speaking*]
  Women, I am ashamed if I appear
  to you too much the mourner with constant dirges.   255
  What I do, I must do. Pardon me. I ask you
  how else would any well-bred girl behave
  that saw the sufferings of her father's house
  as I have seen these, day and night, increasing
  and never a check?   260
  First there's my mother, the one who bore me, now
  a thing of hate. Then in my own house I live
  with those who killed my father. I'm their subject,
  and it's their decision whether I get   265
  or go without.
                  What sort of days do you imagine
  I spend, watching Aegisthus sitting
  on my father's throne, watching him wear
  my father's self-same robes, watching him

at the hearth where he killed him, pouring libations?   270
Watching the ultimate act of insult,
my father's murderer in my father's bed
with my wretched mother—if mother I should call her,
this woman that sleeps with him.
She is so daring that she cohabits with   275
this foul, polluted creature and fears no Fury.
No, as though laughing at what was done,
she has picked out the day on which she killed
my father in her treachery, and on that day
has set a dancing festival and sacrifices   280
sheep, in monthly ritual, "to the gods that saved her."
So within that house I see, to my wretchedness,
the accursed feast named in his honor.
I see it, moan, and waste away, lament—
but only to myself. I may not even cry   285
as much as my heart would have me.
For this woman, all nobility in words,
abuses me: "You godforsaken, hateful thing,
are you the only one whose father is dead?
Is there no one else of humankind in mourning?   290
My curse upon you! May the gods below
grant you from your present sorrows no release!"
Such are her insults, unless she hears from someone
that Orestes is coming. Then she grows quite wild
and stands beside me shrieking: 295
"Aren't you the one responsible for this?
Is not this your doing, you who stole
Orestes from these hands of mine, conveying him
away? But you may be sure you will pay for it
and pay enough." She howls so, and next to her
is her distinguished bridegroom, urging the same,   300
that utter coward, total piece of mischief,
who makes his wars only with women's help.
But I forever wait for Orestes' coming,
to end our troubles. I wait and wait and die.

For his eternal going-to-do-something   305
destroys my hopes, both real and absent.

In such a state, my friends, one cannot
be moderate and restrained, nor pious either.
Evil is all around me, evil
is what I am compelled to practice.

CHORUS LEADER
Tell me, as you talk like this, is Aegisthus here,   310
or is he gone from home?

ELECTRA
                    Certainly, he's gone.
Do not imagine, if he were near, that I
would wander outside. Now he is on his estate.

CHORUS LEADER
If so, I can talk with you with better confidence.   315

ELECTRA
For the present, he is away. What is your wish?

CHORUS LEADER
Tell me: what of your brother? Is he really coming
or hesitating? That is what I want to know.

ELECTRA
He says he is—but does nothing of what he says.

CHORUS LEADER
A man often hesitates when he does a big thing.   320

ELECTRA
I did not hesitate when I rescued him.

CHORUS LEADER
                    Be easy.
He's a noble man and will surely help his friends.   325

ELECTRA
I believe in him, or else had not lived so long.

CHORUS LEADER
Say no more now. I see your sister,
blood of your blood, of the same father and mother,
Chrysothemis, carrying grave-gifts in her hands
such as are usually offered to those below.

(Enter Chrysothemis from the palace.)

CHRYSOTHEMIS
What have you come to say here out of doors,
sister? Will you never learn, in all this time,   330
not to give way to your empty anger?
Yet this much I know, and know my own heart, too,
that I am sick at what I see, so that
if I had strength, I would let them know how I feel.
But under threat of punishment, I think,   335
I must make my voyage with lowered sails,
that I may not seem to be doing something and then
prove ineffectual. I wish you'd do the same.
And yet justice points not where my words are tending,
but where your judgment stands. However, if
I am to live, and not as a prisoner, I must
in all things listen to the ones in power.   340

ELECTRA
It is strange indeed that you who were born
of our father should forget him
and think only of your mother. All these warnings
of me you have learned from her. Nothing is your own.
Now you must make your choice, one way or the other,   345
either to be rash and irrational
or to be sensible—but forget your friends.
Here you are saying: "If I had the strength,
I would show my hatred of them!" Yet, when I
try everything to take vengeance for our father,
you do nothing to help—and even discourage my doing.   350
Doesn't this add cowardice to the list of all our troubles?
Tell me, or let me tell you, what benefit

would I achieve by giving up my mourning?
Do I not live? Yes, I know, badly, but
for me enough. And I hurt them   355
and so give honor to the dead, if there is, there
in that other world, anything that brings pleasure.
But you who tell me you hate them, hate in words only,
while in fact you are living with our father's murderers.

I tell you: never, not though they brought me all those gifts
in which you now feel pride, would I yield to them.   360
Have your rich table and your abundant life;
all the food I need is the quiet of my conscience.
I do not want to win your honor.
Nor would you if you were sound of mind. Now, when you
    could
be called the daughter of the best of fathers,   365
be called instead your mother's. Thus you'll seem to most
a traitor, betraying your friends and your dead father.

CHORUS LEADER
    No anger, I entreat you. In the words of both
    there is value for both, if you, Electra, can   370
    follow her advice and she take yours.

CHRYSOTHEMIS
    Ladies, I am used to her and her words.
    I never would have mentioned this, had not
    I learned of the greatest of misfortunes coming
    her way to put a stop to her long mourning.   375

ELECTRA
    Tell me of your terror. If you can speak to me
    of something worse than my present condition,
    I'll not keep arguing back.

CHRYSOTHEMIS
                    Well, I shall tell you
    everything I know. They plan, if you don't stop

your present mourning, to send you away, to where   380
never a gleam of sun shall visit you.
You shall live out your life in an underground cave
outside this country and there bewail your sorrows.
With this in mind, reflect. And do not blame me
later when you are suffering.
Now is a good time to take thought.

ELECTRA
So this is what they have decided to do with me?   385

CHRYSOTHEMIS
Yes, this exactly, when Aegisthus comes home.

ELECTRA
As far as this goes, let him come home soon.

CHRYSOTHEMIS
Why such a prayer for evil, my poor sister?

ELECTRA
That he may come—if he will do what you say.

CHRYSOTHEMIS
Hoping that *what* may happen to you? Are you crazy?   390

ELECTRA
That I may get away from you all, as far as I can.

CHRYSOTHEMIS
Have you no care of this, your present life?

ELECTRA
Mine is indeed a fine life, to be envied!

CHRYSOTHEMIS
It might be, if you could learn common sense.

ELECTRA
Do not teach me falseness to those I love.   395

CHRYSOTHEMIS
That is not what I teach, but to yield to power.

ELECTRA

Keep practicing that flattery. It is not my way.

CHRYSOTHEMIS

It is a good thing, though, not to fall through stupidity.

ELECTRA

I shall fall, if I must, revenging my father.

CHRYSOTHEMIS

Our father does not blame me for this, I know.   400

ELECTRA

These are the kind of words that cowards praise.

CHRYSOTHEMIS

You will not heed me then? You will not agree?

ELECTRA

No, certainly.
May I not yet be so empty-witted.

CHRYSOTHEMIS

Then I must go on the errand I was sent.

ELECTRA

Where are you going? To whom   405
bringing those offerings?

CHRYSOTHEMIS

My mother sent me with libations for father's grave.

ELECTRA

What are you saying? To her greatest enemy?

CHRYSOTHEMIS

"Whom she herself killed"—you would add.

ELECTRA

Which of her friends persuaded her? Who thought of this?

CHRYSOTHEMIS

I think it was night terrors drove her to it.   410

ELECTRA

Gods of my father, now come to help at last!

CHRYSOTHEMIS

Why do "night terrors" make you confident?

ELECTRA

I'll tell you that when you tell me the dream.

CHRYSOTHEMIS

I cannot tell you much, only a little.

ELECTRA

Tell me it, all the same. A little story   415
has often made or ruined men before now.

CHRYSOTHEMIS

The story goes that she saw my father,
the father that was yours and mine, again
come to life, once more to live with her.
He took and at the hearth planted the scepter   420
which once he bore and now Aegisthus bears,
and up from out this scepter grew a branch
luxuriant with leaves, and shaded all the land
of this Mycenae. This is what I heard
from someone present when she told the Sun
about her dream.   425
                I know no more beyond this
except that it's for her fear she sends me now.
So, by our family's gods, I pray you: listen
to me and do not fall out of stupidity.
For if you reject me, you'll be back again in distress.° 430

ELECTRA

My dear one, not one thing that you are holding
allow to touch that grave, no, nothing!
It would not be god's law nor pious that you
should offer to my father libations

and burial offerings from that enemy woman.
Throw them to the winds! Or hide them deep   435
in the dust, somewhere where no particle of them
may ever reach my father where he lies.
But let them be stored up for her as treasures
below, against the day when *she* shall die.
I tell you, if she were not the most brazen   440
of all of womankind, would she have dared
to pour these enemy libations
over the body of the man she killed?
Consider if you think that the dead man,
as he lies in his grave, will welcome kindly
these offerings from her by whom he was robbed
of life and honor and foully mutilated?   445
And to wash her hands clean she wiped the clots of blood
off onto his head? Can you believe
that these offerings will bring absolution for her murder?
No, no. You let them be. You cut a lock
out of your own hair, from the fringe, and mine,
mine, too, his wretched daughter's. Such a small offering,   450
yet all I have! Give it to him, this rough°
lock of hair, and here, my girdle, unadorned.
Kneel then and pray that from the earth below
he may come himself, a friendly spirit, to help us
against his enemies. Pray that the boy Orestes   455
may live to fight and win against his enemies,
to set his foot upon them. And if so
in days to come we shall be able to dress
this grave with richer hands than we can now.
I think, oh yes, I think that it was he
that thought to send this evil-boding dream   460
to her.

       Yet, sister, do yourself this service
and help me, too, and help the dearest of all,
father of us both, that lies dead in the underworld.

CHORUS LEADER

The girl speaks piously. And you, my dear,
if you are wise, will follow her advice.   465

CHRYSOTHEMIS

I will do it. It is not reasonable for us two
to squabble about what is just. I must haste to do it.
But, my friends, if I attempt this, I must have your silence.
If my mother hears of this, I'm sure I shall regret   470
indeed the attempt that I'm about to make.

(Exit Chrysothemis to the side.)

CHORUS [singing]
                         STROPHE

If I am not a distracted prophet
and lacking in skill of judgment,
Justice foreshadowing the event   475
shall come, in her hands a just victory.
Yes, she will come, my child, in vengeance
and soon:
of that I am confident
since I lately heard   480
of this dream that blows sweet.
Your father, the king of the Greeks,
has never forgotten,
nor the axe of old,
bronze-cast, double-edged,   485
which did him to death
in shame and degradation.

                      ANTISTROPHE

There shall come many-footed, many-handed,
hidden in dreadful ambush,   490
the bronze-shod Fury.
Wicked indeed were they who were seized
with a passion for a forbidden bed,

for a marriage accursed, stained with murder.
In the light of this, I am very sure   495
that never, never shall we see
such a portent draw near without hurt
to doers and partners in crime.
There are indeed no prophecies for mortals
in dreadful dreams and soothsayings
if this night vision come not   500
well and truly to fulfilment.

Horsemanship of Pelops long ago,
loaded with disaster,   505
how deadly you have proved
to this land!
For since the day that Myrtilus
sank to his rest in the sea,
wrecked utterly with the unhappy
wreck of his golden chariot,   510
for never a moment since
has destruction and ruin
ever left this house.   515

(Clytemnestra enters from the palace, with attendants.)

CLYTEMNESTRA

It seems you are loose again, wandering about.
Aegisthus isn't here, who always restrained you
from going abroad and disgracing your family.
But now that he is away you pay no heed
to me, although you have told a lot of people   520
at length how brutally and how unjustly
I lord it over you, insulting
you and yours.
                              There is no insolence in myself,
but being abused by you so constantly
I give abuse in return.

                              Your father, yes,   525
always your father. Nothing else is your pretext—
that he was killed by me. By me. I know it,
well. There is no denial in me. Justice,
justice it was that took him, not I alone.
And you too would have served the cause of justice
if you had been right-minded.

        For this father of yours whom you always mourn,   530
alone of all the Greeks, had the brutality
to sacrifice your sister to the gods,
although he had not toiled for her as I did,
the mother that bore her, he the begetter only.
Tell me, now, why he sacrificed her. Was it   535
for the sake of the Greeks?
But they had no share in my daughter to let them kill her.
Was it for Menelaus' sake, his brother,
that he killed my child? And should he not then pay for it?
Had not this Menelaus two children who
ought to have died rather than mine? It was their parents   540
for whose sake all the Greeks set sail for Troy.
Or had the god of death some longing to feast
on my children rather than hers? Or had
that accursed father lost his love for my children
while feeling it still for those of Menelaus?   545
Was not this the act of a father thoughtless
or with bad thoughts? That is how I see it
even if you differ with me. The dead girl,
if she could speak, would bear me out.
I am not dismayed by all that has happened.
If you think me wicked, keep your righteous judgment   550
and blame your neighbors.

ELECTRA

This is one time you will not be able to say
that the abuse I receive from you was provoked
by something painful on my side.

                              But if
you will allow me I will speak truthfully
on behalf of the dead man and my dead sister.   555

CLYTEMNESTRA

Of course, I allow you. If you always began
our conversations so, you would not be
so painful to listen to.

ELECTRA

                    I will tell you, then.
You say you killed my father. What claim more shameful
than that, whether with justice or without it?   560
But I'll maintain that it was not with justice
you killed him, but the seduction of that evil man,
with whom you now are living, drew you to it.
Ask Artemis the huntress what made her hold
the many winds in check at Aulis. Or
I'll tell you this, since we may not learn from her.   565
My father, as I hear, when at his sport,
started from his feet a horned dappled stag
within the goddess' sanctuary. He
let fly and hit the deer and uttered some boast
about his killing of it. The daughter of Leto   570
was angry at this and so detained the Greeks
in order that my father, to compensate
for the beast killed, would sacrifice his daughter.

Thus was her sacrifice—no other deliverance
for the army either homeward or toward Ilium.
He struggled and fought against it. Finally,   575
constrained, he killed her—not for Menelaus.
But if—I will plead in your own words—he had done so
for his brother's sake, is that any reason
why he should die at your hands? By what law?
If this is the law you lay down for men, take heed   580
you do not lay down for yourself pain and repentance.

If we shall kill one in another's requital,
you would be the first to die, if you met with justice.
No. Think if the whole is not a mere excuse.
Please tell me for what cause you now commit   585
the ugliest of acts—in sleeping with him,
the murderer with whom you first conspired
to kill my father, and breed children to him, and
drive out your former children, honorable ones   590
born of honorable wedlock. What grounds
for praise shall I find in this? Or will you say
that this, too, is retribution for your daughter?
If you say it, still your saying it is scandalous.
It isn't decent to marry with your enemies
even for a daughter's sake.

               But I may not
even rebuke you! What you always say   595
is that it is my mother I am reviling.
Mother! I do not count you mother of mine,
but slave owner and mistress. My life is wretched
because I live with multitudes of sufferings,
inflicted by yourself and your bedfellow.   600
But the other, he is away, he has escaped
your hand, though barely: poor Orestes now
wears out his life in misery and exile.
Many a time you have accused me
of rearing him to be your executioner.
I would have done it if I could. Know that.   605
As far as that goes, you may publicly
proclaim me what you like—traitor, reviler,
a creature full of shamelessness. If I am
naturally skilled at such things, I do no shame
to your nature.

CHORUS LEADER
   I see she is angry, but whether it is in justice,   610
   I no longer see if there's concern for that.

CLYTEMNESTRA

What need have I of concern in her regard
who so insults her mother, though old enough
to know better? Don't you think that she will go
to any lengths, so shameless as she is?   615

ELECTRA

You may be sure I am ashamed of this,
even if you do not think so. I know that
I act improperly, so unlike myself.
But the hate you show for me, and all your actions,
compel me against my will to act this way.   620
For ugly deeds are taught by ugly deeds.

CLYTEMNESTRA

O shameless creature, I and my words and deeds
give you too much to talk of.

ELECTRA

It is you who talk, not I. It is your deeds,
and it's deeds invent the words.   625

CLYTEMNESTRA

Now by the Lady Artemis you shall not escape
the results of your behavior, when Aegisthus comes.

ELECTRA

You see? You let me say what I please, and then
you are outraged. You do not know how to listen.

CLYTEMNESTRA

Hold your peace at least. Allow me to sacrifice,   630
since I have permitted you to say all you will.

ELECTRA

I allow you, yes, I bid you, sacrifice.
Do not blame my tongue; for I will say no more.

CLYTEMNESTRA   (To an attendant.)

Come, do you lift them up, the offerings
of all the fruits of earth, that to this king here   635

I may offer prayers for freedom from my fears.
Phoebus Protector, hear me, as I am,
although the word I speak is muted. Not among friends
is it spoken, nor may I unfold the whole
to the light while this girl stands beside me,
lest with her chattering and malicious tongue   640
she sow in all the city bad reports.
Yet hear me thus, since this is how I will speak.
The dreams of double meaning I have seen
within this night, from them, Lycian king,   645
grant what is good for me prosperous outcome
but what is ill, turn it back upon
those that do us evil.
And if there are some that from my present wealth
plot to expel me with their stratagems,
do not permit them. Let me live out my life,   650
just as my life is now, to the end uninjured,
controlling the house of Atreus and the throne,
living with those I love as I do now,
enjoying prosperity, and with such children
as do not hate me nor cause bitter pain.
These are my prayers, Lycian Apollo; hear them   655
graciously. Grant to all of us what we ask.
For all the rest, although I keep silent,
I know you are a god and know it all.
It is natural that the children of Zeus see all.

(Enter Tutor, from the side.)

TUTOR

Excuse me, ladies, how may I know for certain,   660
is this the palace of the King Aegisthus?

CHORUS LEADER

This is it, sir. Your own guess is correct.

TUTOR

Would I then be right in thinking that this lady
is his wife? She has indeed a royal look.

CHORUS LEADER

Quite right. And here she is for you, herself.

TUTOR

Greetings, Your Majesty. I come with news
from a friend, good news for you and for Aegisthus.

CLYTEMNESTRA

I welcome what you have said. But I would like first
to know who sent you here.

TUTOR

It was Phanoteus
the Phocian, charging me with an important matter. 670

CLYTEMNESTRA

What is it, sir? Please tell me. I know well
you come from a friend and will speak friendly words.

TUTOR

Orestes is dead. There it is, in one short word.

ELECTRA

O no, O no! This is the day I die.

CLYTEMNESTRA

What's this you say, sir, what? Don't listen to her. 675

TUTOR

What I said and say again is "Orestes is dead."

ELECTRA

I am ruined, hopeless—I cannot go on living!

CLYTEMNESTRA *(To Electra.)*

Mind your own business!

(To the Tutor.)

Sir, tell me the truth:
in what way did he meet his death?

This

I was sent to tell, and I will tell you it all.   680
He went to the glorious gathering that Greece holds
in honor of the Delphic Games, and when
he heard the herald's loud proclamation
for the first contest—it was a running race—
he entered, looking brilliant, all eyes upon him.   685
His running was as good as his appearance:
he won the race and came out covered with honor.
There is much I could tell you, but I must tell it briefly.
I have never known a man of such achievement
or prowess. Know this one thing. In all the contests   690
the marshals announced, he won the prize, was cheered,°
proclaimed the victor as "Argive by birth,
by name Orestes, son of Agamemnon,
who once gathered and led the glorious Greek host."   695
So far, so good. But when a god sends ruin,
not even the strong man may escape.

Orestes,

when, the next day, at sunrise, there was a race
for chariot teams, entered with many contestants.   700
There was one Achaean, one from Sparta, two
Libyans, masters in driving racing teams.
Orestes was the fifth among them; he
had as his team Thessalian mares. The sixth
was an Aetolian with young sorrel horses.   705
The seventh was a Magnesian, and the eighth
an Aenian, by race, with a white team.
The ninth competitor came from god-built Athens,
and then a Boeotian, ten chariots in all.
They stood in their allotted stations where   710
the appointed judges placed them. At the signal,
a brazen trumpet, they were off. The drivers called
to their horses, and their hands vibrated the reins,
The course was filled with clamor of rattling chariots.

The dust rose up. The drivers, massed together, 715
applied the goad unsparingly, each one struggling
to advance the nave of his wheel or the snorting mouths
of his horses past his rival, wheels and backs
all slobbered by the breath of the teams behind them.° 720
So far they all stood upright in their chariots.
But the Aenian's hard-mouthed colts got out of hand
and bolted as they finished the sixth lap 725
and turned into the seventh; there they crashed
head-on with the Barcaean chariot. After that,
from this one accident, team crashed team
and overturned each other. All the plain
of Crisa was full of wrecks. But the man from Athens, 730
a clever driver, saw what was happening, pulled
his horses out of the way, and held them in check,
avoiding the disordered mass of teams in the middle.

  Orestes had been driving last and holding
his horses back, putting his trust in the finish. 735
But when he saw the Athenian left alone,
he sent a shrill cry through his swift horses' ears
and set to catch him. The two drove level,
the poles were even. First one, now the other,
would push his horses' heads in front. 740
Orestes always drove tight at the corners
barely grazing the edge of the post with his wheel,
loosening the reins of the trace horse on his right
while he checked the near horse.° In his other laps
the young man and his horses had come through safe.
But this time as he slackened the left rein
while the horse was still turning, unaware, he struck
the edge of the pillar and broke the axle box. 745
He was himself thrown from the rails of the chariot
and tangled in the reins. As he fell, the horses
bolted wildly to the middle of the course.
When the crowd saw him fallen from his chariot,
they cried out with pity for the young man, who'd done 750

such deeds and now was meeting such misfortune,
thrown earthward first, then with legs pointing
to the sky—until at last the charioteers
with difficulty stopped the runaway team
and freed him, but so covered with blood that no one   755
of his friends could have recognized the wretched corpse.
They burned him there on a pyre. Men of Phocis
chosen for the task are bringing in a small urn
of bronze the miserable ashes—all that's left
of this great frame, that he may have his grave   760
here in his father's country.
That is my story,
bitter as stories go, but for us who saw it,
greatest of all misfortunes that I've seen.

CHORUS LEADER
Ah, ah! The ancient family
of our lords has perished, it seems, root and branch.   765

CLYTEMNESTRA
Zeus, what shall I say? Shall I call it good luck?
Or terrible, yet for the best? Indeed,
my state is painful if I must save
my life by means of my own misfortunes.

TUTOR
My lady, why does this story make you dejected?

CLYTEMNESTRA
Mother and child! It is a strange relation.   770
A mother cannot hate the child she bore
even when injured by it.

TUTOR
Our coming here, it seems, then is to no purpose.

CLYTEMNESTRA
Not to no purpose. How can you say "no purpose"—
if you have come with certain proofs of death

of one who from my soul was sprung,   775
but severed himself from my breast, from my nurture, who
became an exile and a foreigner;
who after he quitted this land, never saw me again;
who charged me with his father's murder, threatened
terrors against me. Neither night nor day   780
could I find solace in sleep: each oncoming moment
kept nagging me like one about to die.
But now, with this one day I am freed from fear
of her and him. She was the greater evil;
she lived with me, constantly draining   785
the very blood of life—now perhaps I'll have peace
from her threats. The light of day will come again.

ELECTRA

  Oh no, no! Now must I mourn indeed
  your death, Orestes, when your mother here
  pours insults on you, dead. Can this be right?   790

CLYTEMNESTRA

  Not right for you. But he is right as he is.

ELECTRA

  Hear, Nemesis, of the man that lately died!

CLYTEMNESTRA

  Nemesis has heard what she should, and done things well.

ELECTRA

  Insult us now. For now the luck is yours.

CLYTEMNESTRA

  Will you not stop this, you and Orestes both?   795

ELECTRA

  We are stopped indeed. We cannot make you stop.

CLYTEMNESTRA   *(To the Tutor.)*

  Your coming will be worth much, sir, if you
  have stopped my daughter's everlasting clamor.

TUTOR

Well, I will go now, if all this is settled.

CLYTEMNESTRA

O no! I should do wrong to myself and to   800
the friend who sent you if I let you go.
Please go inside. Leave her out here to wail
the misfortunes of herself and those she loves.

(Exit Clytemnestra and the Tutor into the house.)

ELECTRA

There's an unhappy mother for you! See
how agonized, how bitter, were the tears,   805
how terribly she sorrowed for her son
that met the death you heard of! No, I tell you,
she parted from us laughing. O what misery!
Orestes dearest, your death is my death.
By your passing you have torn away from my heart
whatever solitary hope still lingered   810
that you would live and come some day to avenge
your father and my miserable self.
But now where should I turn? I am alone,
having lost both you and my father. Back again
to be a slave among those I hate most   815
of all the world, my father's murderers!
Is this what is right for me?

                    No, this I will not:
live with them any more. Here, at this gate
I will abandon myself to waste away
this life of mine, unloved. If they're displeased,
let someone kill me, someone that lives within.   820
Death is a favor to me, life an agony.
I have no wish for life.

CHORUS [*singing, with Electra singing in response*]

STROPHE A

Where are Zeus's thunderbolts,
where is the blazing sun,

if they see all this and yet keep it hidden,
holding their peace? 825

CHORUS

Why do you cry, child?

ELECTRA

Ah!

CHORUS

Speak no great word. 830

ELECTRA

You will destroy me.

CHORUS

How?

ELECTRA

If you suggest a hope
when all is plain, when they are gone
to the house of Death, and when I waste 835
my life away, then you are treading me further down.

CHORUS

ANTISTROPHE A
King Amphiaraus, as I know,
was caught by a woman's golden necklace,
and now beneath the earth
reigns over all the spirits there. 840

ELECTRA

Oh, woe!

CHORUS

Woe indeed, for the murderess . . .

ELECTRA

. . . she died!°

CHORUS

Yes.   845

ELECTRA

I know, I know. For him in sorrow
there came a deliverer.
None such for me. For one there was,
but he is gone, snatched away by death.

CHORUS

STROPHE B

Unhappy girl, unhappiness is yours!

ELECTRA

I bear you witness with full knowledge,
knowledge too full, bred of a life,   850
the crowded months surging with horrors
many and dreadful!

CHORUS

We know what you are saying.

ELECTRA

So do not then, I pray you, divert my thoughts to where ...   855

CHORUS

What do you mean?

ELECTRA

... there is no hope, no brother born
of the same noble lineage to help.

CHORUS

ANTISTROPHE B

Death comes to all mortal men.   860

ELECTRA

Yes, but to meet it so,
as he did, poor man,
tangled in the leather reins,
among the wild flurry of hoofs!

CHORUS

    An unwatchable horror!   865

ELECTRA

  True indeed, for he's now a stranger
  that was hidden in earth, by no hand of mine,
  knew no grave I gave him,
  knew no weeping from me.   870

                                       (Enter Chrysothemis.)

CHRYSOTHEMIS

  My dearest sister,
  I am so glad, I have run here in haste,
  regardless of propriety. I bring you
  happiness and a relief from all
  the troubles you have had and sorrowed for.

ELECTRA [*now speaking*]

  Where could you find relief—and who are you   875
  to find it—for my troubles which know no cure?

CHRYSOTHEMIS

  We have Orestes here among us—that is
  my news for you—as plain as you see myself.

ELECTRA

  Are you mad, poor girl, or can it be you laugh
  at what are your own troubles as well as mine?   880

CHRYSOTHEMIS

  I swear by our father's hearth. It is not in mockery
  I speak. He is here in person with us.

ELECTRA

                      Ah!
  Poor girl! Who told you this that you believed him,
  all too credulous?

CHRYSOTHEMIS

        My own eyes were the evidence   885
for what I saw, and no one else.

ELECTRA

                    Poor thing!
What proof was there to see? What did you look at
that has set your heart incurably afire?

CHRYSOTHEMIS

I pray you, hear me by the gods,
and then, having heard me, call me sane or foolish.   890

ELECTRA

Tell me, then, if the story gives you pleasure.

CHRYSOTHEMIS

Yes, I will tell you all I saw.
When I came to our father's ancient grave,
I saw that from the very top of the mound
newly poured streams of milk were flowing, and his tomb   895
was crowned with a wreath of all the flowers
that grow. I saw in wonder, looked about
in case there might be someone near. But when I saw
that all was quiet, I approached the grave.   900
On top of the pyre I saw a fresh-cut lock of hair;
as soon as I saw that, something jumped within me
at the familiar sight. I knew I saw
the token of my dearest, loved Orestes.
I took it in my hands, never saying a word   905
for fear of saying what would be ill-omened,
but in pure joy my eyes were filled with tears.
Both then and now I know with certainty
this offering could come from him alone.
Whom else could this concern, save you and me?
I did not do it, I know, and neither did you.   910
How could you? For you cannot leave this house,

even to worship, but they will punish you for it.
Nor can it be our mother. She is not inclined
to do such things, and if she did, we'd notice it.
These offerings at the grave must be Orestes'. 915
Dear sister, take heart. It is not always the same
fortune that follows anyone. Till now
our fortune was hateful to us. But now perhaps
this day will seal the promise of much good.

ELECTRA

Oh, how I pity you, long since, for your foolishness!

CHRYSOTHEMIS

What is this? Are you not pleased by what I say? 920

ELECTRA

You don't know where you are, nor what you're thinking.

CHRYSOTHEMIS

Why, don't I have knowledge of what I saw quite plainly?

ELECTRA

He is dead, my poor dear. And your rescue at his hands
is dead along with him. Look to him no more. 925

CHRYSOTHEMIS

Alas! From whom on earth did you hear this?

ELECTRA

From one that was near to him, when he was dying.

CHRYSOTHEMIS

Where is that man then? I am lost in wonder.

ELECTRA

He's in the house, as our mother's welcome guest.

CHRYSOTHEMIS

Alas again! But who then would have placed 930
these many offerings on our father's tomb?

ELECTRA

I think perhaps that someone put them there
as a remembrance of the dead Orestes.

CHRYSOTHEMIS

Unlucky I! I was so happy coming,
hurrying to bring my news to you, not knowing   935
what misery we were plunged in. Now when I've come,
I find both our old sorrow and the new.

ELECTRA

That is how things are, yes. But now listen to me,
and you can relieve the suffering that weighs on us.

CHRYSOTHEMIS

So can I bring the dead to life again?   940

ELECTRA

This is not what I mean. I am no such fool.

CHRYSOTHEMIS

What do you bid me do, of which I am capable?

ELECTRA

To have the courage to follow my counsel.

CHRYSOTHEMIS

If I can help at all, I will not refuse.

ELECTRA

Look: there is no success without hardship.   945

CHRYSOTHEMIS

I know. As far as my strength goes, I will help.

ELECTRA

Hear me tell you, then, the plans that I have laid.
Friends to help—you know that we have none:
death has taken them and robbed us. We alone,
the two of us, are left.   950
While I still heard my brother lived and flourished,

I had my hopes that he would come again,
some day, to avenge the murder of our father.
But now that he's no more, I look to you,
that you should not draw back from helping me,
your trueborn sister, kill our father's murderer,   955
Aegisthus.

      There is nothing I should now conceal from you.
What are you waiting for, that you are hesitant?
What hope do you look to, that is still standing?
Now you must sorrow that you have been deprived
of our father's wealth; and you must grieve also   960
that you are growing older, to this point,
without a marriage and a husband. And
don't hope to get them now, for Aegisthus
is not such a fool as to allow children of yours   965
or mine to grow up, obviously to harm him.
But if you follow my plans,
first, you will win from that dead father, gone
to the underworld, and from our brother with him,
the recognition of your piety.
And, secondly, as you were born to freedom,   970
so in the days to come you will be called free
and find a marriage worthy of you: everyone
loves to look to the noble.
Do you not see how great a reputation
you will win for yourself and me by doing this?
For who of citizens and foreigners   975
that sees us will not welcome us with praise:
"These are two sisters. Look, friends, on them well.
They saved their father's house when their enemies
were riding high, and took their stand against murder,
sparing not to risk their lives upon the venture.   980
Therefore, we all should love them, all revere them,
and all at feasts and public ceremonies
honor these two girls for their bravery."
This is what everyone will say of us,

in life and death, to our undying fame. 985
My dear one, hear me. Labor to help your father
and help your brother; give me deliverance
from what I suffer, and deliver yourself, knowing this:
living shamefully, for the nobly born, is shameful.

CHORUS LEADER

In matters like this, forethought is an ally 990
to the one that gives advice and the one that gets it.

CHRYSOTHEMIS

Ladies, before she spoke, if she had good sense,
she would have held to caution; but she has not.

(To Electra.)

Where are you looking, that you arm yourself like this 995
with such audacity and call on me to help?
Can you not see? You are a woman—no man—
and your physical strength is less than is your enemies'!
Their fortune, day by day, grows luckier
while ours declines and comes to nothingness. 1000
Who then, plotting to kill such a man as this,
will escape unharmed and free of all disaster?
We two are now in trouble. Look to it that
we do not get ourselves trouble still worse
if someone hears what you have said.
There is no gain for us, not the slightest help, 1005
to win a noble reputation if
the way to it lies by dishonorable death.
For death is not the worst but when one wants
to die and cannot even have that death.
I beg of you, before you utterly
destroy us and exterminate our family, 1010
check your temper. All that you have said to me
I'll keep, for my part, unspoken and unfulfilled.
Be sensible, you, and, at long last, being weaker,
learn to give in to those that have the strength.

CHORUS LEADER

Follow her advice. There's no greater gain for humans   1015
than prudence and a reasonable mind!

ELECTRA

You have said nothing unexpected. Well
I knew you would reject what I proposed.
The deed must then be done by my own hand
alone. For I won't leave it unattempted.   1020

CHRYSOTHEMIS

Ah!
I would you had felt so when our father died:
you would have carried all before you.

ELECTRA

I was the same in nature then, weaker in judgment.

CHRYSOTHEMIS

Practice to keep that judgment through your life.

ELECTRA

That is advice which means you will not help me.   1025

CHRYSOTHEMIS

Yes—for the attempt most likely brings disaster.

ELECTRA

I envy you your "judgment," but hate your cowardice.

CHRYSOTHEMIS

I will be equally patient when you praise me.

ELECTRA

That you will never experience from me.

CHRYSOTHEMIS

There's a long future to determine that.   1030

ELECTRA

Be gone; for there's no help in you for me.

CHRYSOTHEMIS

There is, but there's no power of learning in you.

ELECTRA

Go and tell all this story to your mother.

CHRYSOTHEMIS

I do not hate you with such a hatred as that.

ELECTRA

Understand, at least, how you dishonor me.   1035

CHRYSOTHEMIS

It is not dishonor, only forethought for you.

ELECTRA

Must I then follow your idea of justice?

CHRYSOTHEMIS

You'll be our leader, once you come to your senses.

ELECTRA

It is terrible to speak well and be wrong.

CHRYSOTHEMIS

A very proper description of yourself.   1040

ELECTRA

What! Don't you think that I say these things with justice?

CHRYSOTHEMIS

There are times when even justice can bring harm.

ELECTRA

These are rules by which I would not wish to live.

CHRYSOTHEMIS

If you make your attempt, you'll find that I am right.

ELECTRA

Yes, I will make it. You will not frighten me.   1045

CHRYSOTHEMIS

Are you sure now? You will not think again?

ELECTRA

No enemy is worse than bad advice.

CHRYSOTHEMIS

You cannot agree with any of what I say?

ELECTRA

I have made my mind up—long ago, in fact.

CHRYSOTHEMIS

I will go away then. You cannot bring yourself°   1050
to approve my words, nor I your disposition.

ELECTRA

Go then. I'll never follow you,
not though you long for it. It is pure folly
to try to pursue vain and empty things.

CHRYSOTHEMIS

Well, if you think that you are right, go on   1055
thinking so. When you are deep in trouble, then
you will agree with what I said.

(Exit Chrysothemis into the palace.)

CHORUS [singing]

STROPHE A

Why, when we see above our heads the birds,
true in their wisdom,
caring for the sustenance   1060
of those that gave them life and help,
why do we not pay our own debts of gratitude so?
But, by Zeus of the lightning bolt,
by Themis, dweller in heaven,
not for long do we go unpunished.   1065
O voice that goes to the dead below,
carry the piteous message
to the Atridae in the underworld,
and tell of wrongs untouched
by joy of the dance.

Tell them that now their house is sick,   1070
tell them that their two children
fight and struggle, that they cannot
any more live in harmony together.
Electra, betrayed, alone,
is down in the waves of sorrow,
constantly bewailing her father's fate,   1075
like the nightingale lamenting.
She takes no thought of death;
she is ready to leave the light
if only she can kill the two Furies.
Was there ever one so noble
born to a father's house?   1080

STROPHE B

Nobody truly good will choose to live
shamefully, if so living
they cloud their renown and die nameless.
O my child, my child, even so you°   1085
have chosen to share the life of mourning,
have rejected dishonor,
to win at once two reputations
as wise and best of daughters.

ANTISTROPHE B

I pray that your life may be lifted high   1090
over your foes,
in wealth and power as much as now
you lie beneath their hand.
For I have found you in distress   1095
but winning the highest prize
by piety toward Zeus
for observance of nature's greatest laws.

(Enter Orestes and Pylades from the side, disguised as Phocian
countrymen and accompanied by attendants who carry an urn.)

ORESTES

I wonder, ladies, if we were directed right
and have come to the destination that we sought?

CHORUS LEADER

What do you seek? And what do you want here?   1100

ORESTES

I have asked all the way here where Aegisthus lives.

CHORUS LEADER

You have arrived and need not blame your guides.

ORESTES

Would some one of you be so kind to tell
the household we have come, a welcome company?

CHORUS LEADER

This lady, as nearest of kin, could bear the message.   1105

ORESTES

Then, lady, will you please report within
that certain men of Phocis seek Aegisthus.

ELECTRA

O no! Then are you bringing the certain proofs
of those rumors we received before you came?

ORESTES

I do not know about rumor. Old Strophius sent me   1110
here to bring news about Orestes.

ELECTRA

What is it, sir? How fear steals over me!

ORESTES

Within this little urn, as you can see,
we are bringing home his small remains. He is dead.

ELECTRA

Ah, ah! This is it indeed, all clear.   1115
Here is my sorrow visible, before me.

ORESTES

If you are one that sorrows for Orestes
and his troubles, know this urn contains his body.

ELECTRA

Sir, give it to me, by the gods. If he
is hidden in this urn—give it into my hands,   1120
that I may weep and cry lament together
for myself and my whole family with these ashes.

ORESTES [*speaking to his attendants*]

Bring it and give it to her, whoever she is.
It is not in enmity she asks for it.
One of his friends, no doubt, or of his blood.   1125

                    (*The attendants do as directed.*)

ELECTRA [*speaking*]   (*To the urn.*)

Precious memorial of my dearest love,
my most loved in the world, all that remains
of live Orestes, oh, how differently
from the hopes I sent you with do I receive you home!
Now all I hold of you is nothingness;
but you shone brilliantly, child, when from this house
I sent you forth.   1130
Would that I had left life before I sent you
abroad to a foreign country, when I stole you
with these two hands, saved you from being murdered.
Then on that very day you would have died,
and lying there would have found your share,   1135
your common portion of your father's grave.
Now far from home, an exile, on alien soil
without your sister near, you died unhappily.
I did not, to my sorrow, wash you with
these hands that loved you, did not lift you up,
as was my right, a weight of misery,   1140
from the fierce blaze of the pyre. The hands of strangers
gave you your rites, and so you come again,
a tiny weight enclosed in a tiny vessel.

Alas for all my nursing of long ago,
so constant—all for nothing—which I gave you   1145
with such sweet trouble. For you never were
as much your mother's love as you were mine;
none was your nurse but I within that household,
and I was always the one called "sister." Now
in one day all that is gone—for you are dead:
all, all you have snatched with you in your going, like   1150
a hurricane. Our father is dead and gone.
I am dead in you; and you are dead yourself.
Our enemies laugh. Frantic with joy she grows,
mother, no mother, the one you promised me
in secret messages so often you   1155
would come to punish. Now our evil fortune,
yours and mine, has stolen all this away,
and sent you back to me like this—no longer
the form I used to love, only your dust
and idle shade.

[*singing*]
Ah, ah!!

O body pitiable! Ah!   1160
O saddest journey that you went, my love,
and so have destroyed me! Ah!
O brother, loved one, you have destroyed me!

[*now speaking again*]
Therefore, receive me to your habitation,   1165
nothing to nothing, that with you below
I may dwell from now on. When you were on earth,
I shared all with you equally. Now I claim
in death no less to share a grave with you.
The dead, I see, no longer suffer pain.   1170

CHORUS LEADER
Think, Electra, your father was mortal, and mortal
was Orestes also. Do not sorrow too much.
This is a debt that all of us must pay.

[96] SOPHOCLES

ORESTES
Ah!
What shall I say? What words can I use? It's impossible;
I am no longer master of my tongue.   1175

ELECTRA
What ails you? What is the meaning of your words?

ORESTES
Is this the glorious form of Electra that I see?

ELECTRA
Yes. This is she; and truly miserable.

ORESTES
Alas for this most lamentable event!

ELECTRA
Is it for me, sir, you are sorrowing?   1180

ORESTES
That body, so cruelly and godlessly abused!

ELECTRA
None other than myself must be the subject
of your ill-omened words, sir.

ORESTES
                                        O, alas
for your life without husband or happiness!

ELECTRA
Why do you look at me so, sir? Why lament?

ORESTES
How little then I knew of my own troubles!   1185

ELECTRA
From what that has been said did you learn this?

ORESTES
I see you and your sufferings, so conspicuous.

ELECTRA

It's little of my suffering that you see.

ORESTES

How can there be things worse to see than this?

ELECTRA

Because I live with those that murdered him.   1190

ORESTES

Murderers? Whose? Where is this evil you hint at?

ELECTRA

My father's murderers; and I'm forced to be their slave.

ORESTES

Who is it that forces you to such subjection?

ELECTRA

She is called my mother—but she's like a mother in nothing.

ORESTES

How does she compel you? Hardship or violence?   1195

ELECTRA

With violence and hardship and all ills.

ORESTES

You have no one to help you or prevent her?

ELECTRA

No. There was one. You have shown me his dust.

ORESTES

Poor girl! When I look at you, how I pity you!

ELECTRA

Then you are the only one that ever pitied me.   1200

ORESTES

Yes. I alone came here and felt your pain.

ELECTRA

You haven't perhaps come from somewhere as our kinsman?

ORESTES

I will tell you—if these women here are friends.

ELECTRA

Yes, friends indeed. You may speak quite freely.

ORESTES

Give up this urn then, and you shall know all.   1205

ELECTRA

Don't make me do that, stranger—by the gods!

ORESTES

Do what I bid you. You will not be wrong.

ELECTRA

By your beard! Do not rob me of what I love most!

ORESTES

I will not let you keep it.

ELECTRA

O Orestes!
Alas, if I may not even give you burial!   1210

ORESTES

No words of ill omen! You have no right to mourn.

ELECTRA

Have I no right to mourn for my dead brother?

ORESTES

You have no right to call him by that title.

ELECTRA

Am I then so dishonored in his sight?

ORESTES

No one dishonors you. But this is not for you.   1215

ELECTRA

It is—if it's Orestes' body that I hold here.

ORESTES

But it's not Orestes'—except in make-believe.

ELECTRA

Where is the poor boy buried then?

ORESTES

                              Nowhere.
There is no grave for living men.

ELECTRA

                              How, boy,
what do you mean?

ORESTES

                  Nothing that is untrue.   1220

ELECTRA

Is he alive then?

ORESTES

                  Yes, if I am living.

ELECTRA

And are you he?

ORESTES

                  Look at this signet ring
that was our father's, and know if I speak true.

ELECTRA

O happiest light!

ORESTES

                  Happiest I say, too.

ELECTRA

Voice, have you come?

ORESTES

                  Hear it from no other source.   1225

ELECTRA

Do my arms hold you?

ORESTES

Never again to part.

ELECTRA

Dearest of women, fellow citizens,
here is Orestes that was dead by contrivance,
and now by contrivance is restored to life again!

CHORUS LEADER

We see, my child, and at your happy fortune   1230
tears of gladness trickle from our eyes.

ELECTRA [singing, while Orestes speaks]

STROPHE

Child of the body that I loved the best,
at last you have come,
you have come, you have found, you have seen those you
yearned for.

ORESTES

Yes, I have come. But bide your time in silence.   1235

ELECTRA

Why?

ORESTES

Silence is better, that none inside may hear.

ELECTRA

No, by Artemis, ever virgin,
this I will never stoop to fear—
the women who live inside,   1240
a vain burden on the earth.

ORESTES

Yes, but consider that in women too
there lives a warlike spirit. You have proof of it.

ELECTRA

Ah, indeed!   1245
You have awakened our sorrow
the nature of which no cloud can cover,
nothing can undo,
no forgetfulness overcome,
our sorrow in all its evil.   1250

ORESTES

I know that too. But when the right moment comes,
then will be the time to remember what was done.

ELECTRA

ANTISTROPHE
Every moment, every moment of all time
would justly suit my complaints.   1255
For hardly now are my lips free of restraint.

ORESTES

And I agree. Therefore, hold fast that freedom.

ELECTRA

By doing what?

ORESTES

Where there is no occasion,
do not choose to talk too much.

ELECTRA

Who could find a fit bargain   1260
of words for such silence,
now you have appeared?
Past hope, past calculation,
I see you now.

ORESTES

You see me when the gods moved me to come.°

. . . .

ELECTRA

> You tell me then of a grace surpassing
> what I knew before, if in very truth
> the gods have given you to this house.
> This I do count an action divine.

1270

ORESTES

Indeed, I hesitate to check your joy;
only I fear your pleasure may be too great.

ELECTRA

EPODE

> Orestes, you have come at last,
> have made the journey worth all the world to me,
> have come before me at last.
> Now that I see you
> after so much sorrow,
> do not, I beg you ...

1275

ORESTES

What should I not do?

ELECTRA

> ... do not deprive me
> of the joy of seeing your face.

ORESTES

I would be angry if I saw this in anyone else.

ELECTRA

> You agree?

ORESTES

Of course I do.

1280

ELECTRA

> My dear one, I have heard your voice,
> the voice I never hoped to hear.
> Till now I have held my rage speechless;°

I did not cry out when I heard bad news.
But now I have you. You have come,   1285
your dearest face before me
that even in suffering I could never forget.

ORESTES

Spare me all superfluity of speech.
Tell me not how my mother is villainous,
nor how Aegisthus drains my father's wealth   1290
by luxury and waste. Words about this
will shorten time and opportunity.
But tell me what we need for the present moment,
how openly or hidden by our coming now
we can put a stop to our enemies' mockery.   1295
And take care that our mother does not realize
by your radiant face, when we two go inside.
Keep groaning over my destruction, as it was
emptily described in words. For when we have triumphed,
then you may freely show your joy, and laugh.   1300

ELECTRA [*now speaking*]

Brother, your pleasure shall be mine. These joys
I have from you; they are not mine to own.
I would not agree to hurt you in the slightest,
even if this would bring great profit for myself.   1305
If I did so, I would not properly
be serving the god who watches over us.
       You know the situation. You have heard
Aegisthus is not at home; our mother is.
And don't be afraid that she will see my face   1310
radiant with smiles: our hatred is too old,
I am too steeped in it. And since I have seen you,
my tears of joy will still run readily.
How can they cease when on the selfsame day
I have seen you dead and then again alive?   1315
For me your coming is a miracle,
so that if my father should come back to life

I would think it no wonder but believe
I saw him. Since your coming is such for me,
lead as you will. Had I been all alone,
I would not have failed to win one of two things,   1320
a noble deliverance or a noble death.

ORESTES

Hush, hush! I hear one of the people within
coming out.

ELECTRA

        Please enter our house, dear guests—
more so, since what you are carrying in is that
which no one would refuse—nor be delighted,
if he receives it.   1325

TUTOR   *(Entering from the palace.)*
                 Fools and madmen! No
concern for your own lives at all? No sense
to realize that you are not merely near
the deadliest danger, but in its very midst?   1330
If I had not, this while past, stood guard here
at the door, your plans would now be in the house
before your bodies. I and only I
took the precautions. Have done once and for all
with your long speeches, your insatiable   1335
cries of delight, and in with you at once!
As we are now, delay is ruinous:
it is high time to have done with our task.

ORESTES

How's everything inside, as I go in?

TUTOR

Well. There is no chance of your recognition.   1340

ORESTES

You have announced my death, I understand.

TUTOR

You are down in Hades, as far as they're concerned.

ORESTES

Were they glad of it? Or what did they say?

TUTOR

I will tell you at the end. As things are now,
all on their side is well—even what is not so.   1345

ELECTRA

Brother, who is this man? I beg you, tell me.

ORESTES

Do you not know him?

ELECTRA

                    I cannot even guess.

ORESTES

Do you not know him to whose hands you gave me?

ELECTRA

What, this man?

ORESTES

                    By his hands and by your forethought
I was conveyed away to Phocian country.   1350

ELECTRA

Is this the man, alone among so many,
whom I found loyal when our father was murdered?

ORESTES

This is he. There is no need for further questions.

ELECTRA

O light of day most loved! O only rescuer
of Agamemnon's house, how did you come   1355
back here? Are you indeed that man who saved
both Orestes and me from so many dangers?

O most loved hands, service of feet most kind!
To think you were standing beside me for so long,
and I didn't know you, and you gave no sign!
You killed me with your words while in reality
you were bringing sweet joy. Bless you, my father—   1360
for I think I see a father in you. Blessings!
Within a single day, of all mankind
I have most hated and loved you most.

TUTOR

Enough, I think. As for the story
of the happenings in between, there'll be many days   1365
and nights, as time comes round, to tell you all
clearly, Electra.

(To Orestes and Pylades.)

But as you two stand here
I say to you: now is your chance to act.
Clytemnestra is alone. No man is within.
If you hold back now, you will have others to fight   1370
more clever and more numerous than these.

ORESTES

Pylades, our need now is not for lengthy speeches,
but to get inside as quick as ever we can,
only first saluting the ancestral gods
whose statues stand beside the forecourt here.   1375

(Orestes, Pylades, and the Tutor exit into the palace.)

ELECTRA

Apollo, Lord, give gracious ear to them
and to me, too, that often made you offerings,
out of such store as I had, with prayerful hand.
So now, Lycian Apollo, I kneel before you,
I pray and entreat you, with all the resources   1380
that I possess: please be kind to us,
help us in the fulfilment of our plans

and demonstrate to all mankind the punishment
the gods exact for wickedness.

(Exit Electra into the palace.)

CHORUS [*singing*]

STROPHE A
See how the war god approaches,
breathing bloody vengeance, invincible Ares. 1385
They have gone under the roof of the house now,
those pursuers of evil crimes,
hounds that none may escape;
so that the dream that hung hauntingly
in my mind shall not wait long for fulfilment. 1390

ANTISTROPHE A
Stealthy, stealthy-footed, into the house
he goes, the champion of dead men,
into his father's palace rich from of old,
holding the blade of blood,
new-whetted, in his hands. Hermes,
the child of Maia, hiding the crafty deed in darkness, 1395
conducts him to its end, and delays not.

(Electra enters from the palace.)

ELECTRA [*mostly speaking, while Orestes speaks in response*]

STROPHE B
Dear friends, now is the moment that the men
are finishing their work. Wait in silence.

CHORUS LEADER
What do you mean? What are they doing?

ELECTRA

                                    She is preparing 1400
the urn for burial, and they stand beside her.

CHORUS LEADER
Why have you hurried out here?

ELECTRA

> To watch
that Aegisthus does not come on them unawares.

CLYTEMNESTRA   *(Cries out from within the palace.)*
House, O house
deserted by friends, full of killers!   1405

ELECTRA
Someone cries out, inside. Do you hear?

CHORUS [*singing*]
What I hear is a terror to the ear.
I shudder at it.

CLYTEMNESTRA   *(Cries out again from within.)*
Oh! Oh! Aegisthus, where are you?

ELECTRA
Again, that cry!

CLYTEMNESTRA
> My son, my son,   1410
pity your mother!

ELECTRA
> You had none for him,
nor for his father that begot him.

CHORUS [*singing*]
> City,
and miserable family, now
that day-to-day fate of yours is coming to an end.°

CLYTEMNESTRA
Oh! I am struck!

ELECTRA
> If you have strength—again!

CLYTEMNESTRA
Once more! Oh!   1415

ELECTRA

> If only Aegisthus were with you!

CHORUS [*singing*]

> *The curses are being fulfilled;*
> *those under the earth are alive;*
> *men long dead draw from their killers*
> *blood to answer blood.*   1420

> *(Enter Orestes and Pylades from the palace.)*

CHORUS LEADER° [*now speaking*]

> ANTISTROPHE B
> And here they come. The bloody hand drips
> with Ares' sacrifice. I cannot blame them.

ELECTRA

> Orestes, how have you fared?

ORESTES

> In the house, all
> is well, if Apollo prophesied well.   1425

ELECTRA

> Is the wretched woman dead?

ORESTES

> You need fear no more
> that your mother's arrogance will dishonor you.°

CHORUS [*singing*]

> *Stop! I can see Aegisthus*
> *clearly coming this way.*

ELECTRA

> Boys, back to the house!   1430

ORESTES

> Where do you see him?

ELECTRA

He's in our power,
walking toward us from the suburb, full of joy.

CHORUS [*singing*]

Back to the vestibule, quick as you can.
You have done one part well; now here is the other.

ORESTES

Don't worry, we will do it.   1435

ELECTRA

                              Go

where you will, then.

ORESTES

                    See, I am gone.

ELECTRA

Leave what is here to me.

                          (*Exit Orestes into the palace with Pylades.*).

CHORUS [*singing*]

A few words spoken softly in his ear
would be good, that unawares
he may rush into his contest against Justice.   1440

                          (*Enter Aegisthus from the side.*)

AEGISTHUS

Which of you knows where the Phocian visitors are?
I am told they are come here with news for me
that Orestes met his end in a chariot wreck.
You there, yes, I mean you, who formerly   1445
were so bold and insolent; I should think
it is you this news concerns the most, and therefore
you will know best to tell it to me.

ELECTRA

I know it, of course. Were it not so, I would be
an outsider to what concerns my best beloved.

AEGISTHUS

Where are the strangers then? Tell me that.   1450

ELECTRA

Inside. They have found a very generous hostess.

AEGISTHUS

And do they genuinely report his death?

ELECTRA .

Better than that. They have brought himself, not news.

AEGISTHUS

Can I then see the body in plain sight?

ELECTRA

You can indeed. It is an unenviable sight.   1455

AEGISTHUS

What you say delights me—an unusual thing!

ELECTRA

You may delight, if you find these things delightful.

AEGISTHUS   *(To the servants.)*

Open the doors, I command you, for all to see,°
all Mycenaeans and Argives, and if there's anyone
who formerly had raised up empty hopes   1460
for Orestes, now he may look on the dead
and so accept my bridle, and thus avoid
a more forcible encounter with myself
and punishment to make him grow some sense.

ELECTRA

I have done everything on my side. At long last
I have learned some sense, agreement with the stronger.   1465

> *(The doors of the palace are opened, to reveal a covered body
> on a bier, with Orestes and Pylades standing in front of it.)*

AEGISTHUS

    O Zeus, I see a revelation that has happened
    not without the gods' anger. Or if that is something
    I should not say, because of Nemesis,
    I take it back. Lift all the covers from
    that face, so kinship at least may have due mourning.

ORESTES

    Handle it yourself. This is not mine,   1470
    it's yours—to see and greet with loving words.

AEGISTHUS

    True. I accept that. And you, will you call
    Clytemnestra, if she is at home?

ORESTES

                       She is near you.
    You need not look elsewhere.

AEGISTHUS   *(Lifting the covering.)*
                   What do I see?   1475

ORESTES

    Something you fear? Do you not know the face?

AEGISTHUS

    Who are these men that have driven me into their net
    to my destruction?

ORESTES

                Did you take so long
    to find that your names are all astray
    and those you call the dead are living?

AEGISTHUS

                Ah!
    I understand. And you who speak to me   1480
    can only be Orestes.

ORESTES

Were you, so good a prophet, so long misled?

AEGISTHUS

This is my end then. But let me say one thing,
one short word.

ELECTRA

I beg you, brother; don't let him draw out the talking.
When men are in the middle of trouble, when one°   1485
is on the point of death, how can time matter?
Kill him as quickly as you can; and when you've killed him,
throw him out to find such burial as suits him,
out of our sights. This is the only thing for me
that can bring release from sufferings long endured.   1490

ORESTES   (To Aegisthus.)

In with you, then. It is not words that now
are the issue, but your life.

AEGISTHUS

Why into the house?
Why do you need the dark if what you do
is fair? Why is your hand not ready to kill me?

ORESTES

You are not to give orders. Go in, where you killed   1495
my father, so you may die in the same place!

AEGISTHUS

Is it completely necessary that this house
see the evils of the Pelopidae, now and to come?

ORESTES

Yours, at least. Of that I am an excellent prophet.

AEGISTHUS

Your father did not have the skill you boast of.   1500

ORESTES

Too many words! You are slow to take your road.
Go now.

AEGISTHUS

You lead the way.

ORESTES

No, you go first.

AEGISTHUS

Afraid that I'll escape you?

ORESTES

No, but you shall not
die as you choose. I must take care that death
is bitter for you. Justice shall be taken°   1505
directly on all who act above the law—
justice by killing. So we would have less crime.

(Exit Aegisthus into the palace, followed by
Orestes, Pylades, and Electra.)

CHORUS [chanting]
O family of Atreus, how many sufferings
were yours before you came at last so hardly
to freedom, by this day's deed perfected.   1510

IPHIGENIA AMONG THE TAURIANS

EURIPIDES
Translated by Anne Carson

INTRODUCTION TO EURIPIDES' IPHIGENIA AMONG THE TAURIANS

The date of this play is uncertain, but approximately 414 BCE is a fairly safe guess.

The story involves two important variants on the legend of the House of Atreus: the transportation of Iphigenia to the Tauric Chersonese on the northern coast of the Black Sea to serve as a priestess of Artemis; and the last wanderings of Orestes, which unite him with his lost sister. These variants are clearly explained in the text, at lines 1-41 and 940-78, respectively.

Iphigenia among the Taurians is technically a tragedy, that is, a serious play in elevated poetical language presented on the occasion when tragedies were produced. But in the modern sense of the term it is not "tragic." It has often been called "romantic comedy," of a type also exemplified in Euripides' *Helen*, his *Ion*, and many lost plays by various Greek dramatists. It is not merely a matter of the happy ending. Other tragedies have that. But here the emphasis is, even more than usually, on plot, on the how rather than the why of the story. Danger hovers; there is excitement, and pathos, but no catastrophe; the first climax comes in recognition, the second in escape. The plot is excellent indeed, and the mechanism of the recognition scene is brilliantly contrived; in Aristotle's view, it was one of the finest tragedies ever written.

IPHIGENIA AMONG THE TAURIANS

Characters   IPHIGENIA, daughter of Agamemnon
and Clytemnestra; priestess of Artemis
ORESTES, son of Agamemnon and
Clytemnestra
PYLADES, friend of Orestes
CHORUS of captive Greek women
TAURIAN HERDSMAN
THOAS, king of the Taurians
MESSENGER, a servant of Thoas
ATHENA

*Scene: The entrance to the temple of Artemis in the land of the
Taurians, with a large, bloodstained altar in front of it.*

                        (Enter Iphigenia from the temple.)

IPHIGENIA
    Pelops son of Tantalus came to Pisa on swift horses
    and married Oenomaus' daughter
    who begot Atreus.
    Atreus begot Menelaus and Agamemnon.
    Agamemnon begot me.
    I am Iphigenia, daughter of the daughter of Tyndareus.   5
    My father killed me—
    at Euripus where stiff breezes
    spin the salt-blue sea in spirals,
    for Helen's sake

a sacrifice to Artemis in famous Aulis—
or so people think.

        For at Aulis Agamemnon   10
had assembled a thousand ships,
a Greek expedition to take the crown of Troy.
He wanted the Greeks to avenge Helen's rape
and gratify Menelaus.
What befell him was the disaster of windlessness.
He resorted to divination
and Calchas said this: 15
"Agamemnon, commander of this Greek army,
not one ship will cast off from this shore
until Artemis receives your own girl
Iphigenia
as a sacrifice.
You made a vow once   20
to Artemis Lightbringer to offer up
the finest fruit of that year
and that year
your wife bore a child in the house—"
that "finest fruit" was me!
"Her you must kill."

        So Odysseus planned it:
they got me from my mother on pretext of marrying Achilles.   25
And I came to Aulis—sad day for me!
Lifted high above the altar I was right on the verge of death
when Artemis snatched me,
put a deer in my place.
Sent me clear through the air to the land of the Taurians: here!   30
The land is barbarian, so is the king—Thoas
(his name means "swift" and he is).
The goddess put me here in her temple as priestess.
And there's a ritual°   35
beautiful in name only,
that Artemis finds pleasing—well,

I won't say more. She terrifies me.
The fact is, by a law of the city older than me
I sacrifice any Greek man who comes here.
That is, I start things off. Others do the killing. 40
Inside the temple.
We don't talk about this.

New strange dreams came in the night.
I shall tell them—it might bring relief.
In my dream it seemed I'd gone from this land to live in
    Argos. 45
I was lying asleep in a room of girls
when the earth gave a jolt.
I fled, stood outside, saw the cornice falling
and the whole roof collapse to the ground in a heap.
One pillar remained of our ancestral home: 50
I saw it grow blonde hair and speak a human voice.
Then putting my stranger-killing skills to use
I began sprinkling water
as on one about to die.
And I was weeping.
Here's how I read this dream: 55
Orestes is dead, it was him I sprinkled with water.
Boys are the pillars of a house, are they not,
and anyone I consecrate does die.°
So I want to offer libations to my brother. 60
He and I are far apart
but this at least I can do.
I'll go with my women—Greeks given me by the king.
For some reason they're not here yet.
I shall go into the temple—that's where I live. 65

                (Exit Iphigenia into the temple.
            Enter Orestes and Pylades from the side.)

ORESTES
    Look, be careful. Might be someone on the path.

PYLADES

Yes, I'm peering in every direction.

ORESTES

Pylades, does this look to you like the goddess' temple,
the one we sailed here from Argos to find? 70

PYLADES

Yes it does, Orestes.

ORESTES

And this is the altar, wet with Greek blood?

PYLADES

The top of it anyway is bloodstained red.

ORESTES

And do you see spoils hanging from the top?

PYLADES

Spoils from foreigners who died here. 75
But I think I should take a good look around.

ORESTES

O Phoebus, what is this net you have led me into?
Your oracle bid me avenge my father's blood
by killing my mother
but relays of Furies
came hounding me from my land 80
and after I'd run lap after lap on their turning track
I came to you, asked how to find my way out
of wheeling madness and pain.°
You told me to go to the Taurian land 85
where your sister Artemis has her altars
and steal a statue of the goddess
that (people say) fell from the sky to this temple here.
Take it by cunning or take it by luck, no matter the risk, 90
and give it to Athens.
That's all you said.

If I do this, I breathe free.
So
I obeyed you, I came here.
To a land unknown and inhospitable.
But, Pylades, tell me, what should we do?   95
You're my partner in this.
You see those high encircling walls?
Should we mount ladders?
But won't we be seen? Or force the bolts with crowbars?°
But we know of no crowbars.
And if we're caught opening the gates   100
or devising a way in, we're dead.
Let's just run for it, before we get killed—
we can use the same boat we came on.

PYLADES

To run is unacceptable. We're not like that.
And the oracle of god must be respected.   105
Let's quit this temple and go hide in the caves
where the dark seawater washes in.
We'll keep our distance from the ship
in case someone sees it, reports us and has us arrested.
And as soon as the eye of night darkens   110
we must nerve ourselves to steal that statue from the temple
any way we can.°
Good men find the nerve for ordeals, cowards are nothing.°   115

ORESTES

You're right, yes, we should hide out somewhere.
It won't be my fault if the god's oracle goes unfulfilled.   120
We will find the nerve!
Young men have no excuse shirking hard work!

(Exit Orestes and Pylades to one side. Enter the Chorus
of captive Greek women from the other side.)

CHORUS° [*singing*]
   Silence!

O you who dwell by the Clashing Rocks and the Hostile Sea!   125
O Dictynna,
child of Leto, wild as mountains,
to your court, to your gold columns I come,
a pure holy girl on pure holy feet,   130
serving the one who holds your holy key,
I who have lost the towers and walls of Greece rich in horses,
lost the groves and grasslands of Europe,   135
lost the halls of my father,
here I am.
Tell me your news, tell me your troubles.
Why have you brought me, brought me to the temple,
O child of the man
who came against the towers of Troy
with a glorious fleet of a thousand ships
and ten thousand glorious men?°   140

(Enter Iphigenia from the temple.)

IPHIGENIA [singing in this lyric interchange with the Chorus, who
continue to sing in reply]
My ladies!
I'm oppressed by the pain of lament,   145
by lyreless unmusical music,
by keening.
Ruin comes at me.
I grieve for my brother—
such a vision I saw in the night just past.°   150
I am lost.
Am lost.
Our house is no more.
Our family gone.   155
What sorrows swept Argos!
O god, you god,
who rob me of my only brother
by sending him down to death.
For him I pour out these libations

and a mixing bowl to wet the earth—   160
milk of mountain cows,
wine of Bacchus,
honey of yellow bees,
these I pour.
They comfort the dead.   165

Now hand me that vessel of gold,
libation for the god of death.

O child of Agamemnon under the ground,   170
these are for you.
Receive them.
I'll not be bringing bright locks of hair to crown your tomb,
I'll not be bringing tears.
I am far far away from our homeland, yours and mine,   175
and the people there think I am butchered and dead.

CHORUS
Mistress,
I'll sing you antiphonies,
the rough raw noise of Asian songs,   180
dirges for the dead—
what Hades sings—the opposite of paeans.   185
Pity the house of Atreus!
Gone is its light, its scepter.
Gone is the pomp of all those brilliant kings.°   190
Trouble rushes on trouble.
One day in a whirl of winged horses
the Sun changed course
and turned his holy face away.
Then sorrow upon sorrow came to the house of the golden lamb,   195
killing on killing, grief on grief:
from all that ancient Tantalid wrong   200
punishment unfolds now.
And the god is zealous against you.

IPHIGENIA
    From the beginning my luck was unlucky.°
    Right from my mother's womb, that first night,   205
    the Fates wove an absolute education for me.
    I was the firstborn of Leda's poor daughter,   210
    victim of a father's atrocity,
    an offering that brought no joy.°
    They rode me in chariots over Aulis' sands—   215
    a bride!
    Pity me—I was no bride! Bride of Achilles,
    alas!
    Now I live as a stranger in a barren house by the Hostile Sea.
    I've no marriage, no children, no city, no loved ones.   220
    Once the Greeks wooed me.°   208
    I no longer sing songs for Hera at Argos,   221
    I no longer weave Athenas and Titans
    to the hum of the loom.
    No, I work in blood—making death for strangers°   225
    who cry out for pity, who shed tears for pity.
    I give not a thought to them now.   230
    It's my brother I weep, killed in Argos.
    Him I left a mere infant,
    a baby, a young thing, a tendril in his mother's hands,
    at his mother's breast:
    the rightful scepter-bearing king of Argos, Orestes.   235

                      (Enter Herdsman from the side.)

CHORUS LEADER
    But look, here comes a herdsman
    heading up from the shore with news for you.

HERDSMAN
    Child of Agamemnon and Clytemnestra,
    listen to my strange report.

IPHIGENIA [*now speaking*]
    What strange report?   240

HERDSMAN
New arrivals—two young men—have come to our land.
Their boat escaped the dark-blue Clashing Rocks.
What a welcome contribution to our goddess!
Get your holy water ready and your consecrations.   245

IPHIGENIA
Where are they from? What do they look like?

HERDSMAN
Greeks. That's all I know.

IPHIGENIA
You heard no names?

HERDSMAN
One called the other Pylades.

IPHIGENIA
What about his companion?   250

HERDSMAN
Didn't hear, don't know.

IPHIGENIA
Where did you catch them?

HERDSMAN
Down by the edge of the Hostile Sea.

IPHIGENIA
What are herdsmen doing down by the sea?

HERDSMAN
Bathing our oxen in salt water.   255

IPHIGENIA
Go back to the question
where you caught them and how.
This I want to know.
It's been a long time since the goddess' altar ran red with
    Greek blood.°

HERDSMAN

Well, we were driving our oxen into the water that flows   260
out through the Clashing Rocks.
There was a cleft drilled through by the beat of the sea
where purplefishers shelter.
Here one of us caught sight of two young men.
He came back on tiptoe and said   265
"Look—gods sitting there!"
Another (a pious fellow) lifted his hands to pray:
"Son of sea goddess Leucothea, protector of ships,   270
lord Palaemon, be gracious—
whether those are the twin sons of Zeus there
or some sweet offspring of Nereus
who bore the fifty dancing daughters!"
Then a bold skeptical fellow laughed at the prayers   275
and said it was two shipwrecked sailors
sitting terrified in the cleft—"no doubt they've heard we
   slaughter strangers."
This made sense to most of us.
We decided to take them for the goddess to sacrifice
as per usual.
Meanwhile
one of the strangers came out of the cave. He stood.   280
He tossed his head up and down, howling aloud,
trembling to the tips of his fingers
and staggering in fits.
He cried out like a hunter, "See that one, Pylades?
And there, that snake of hell—look, she's itching to kill me,   285
her horrible snakes are mouthing out at me.
And this one's belching fire and death and thrashing her
   wings,°
she's got a stone shaped like my mother in her arms—
she's going to hurl it!   290
Help, she'll kill me! Where can I run?"

Yet those shapes were not visible.

Only voices of cows and dogs were answering him.°
And we for our part, expecting him to die any minute,
sat crouched in silence.   295
But he drew his sword, leapt among the cattle like a lion
and began laying about him, his blade striking flank and rib,
fantasizing he was driving off the Furies.°
The sea bloomed red with blood.   300
And now
seeing the slaughter of the cows
everyone began to arm himself
and we blew conches to summon the locals
(figuring cowherds were no match for these strong young
    foreigners).   305
We soon had a crowd.
But the stranger let go the pulse of his frenzy
and dropped to the ground.
Foam dripped off his chin.
We all set to work on him, pelting and pounding,
while the other man kept trying to wipe off the foam   310
and shield his friend's body with his cloak,
warding off wounds
and ministering to his friend every way he could.

Now the stranger
all of a sudden sane
jumped up.   315
Saw the tide of foes falling on them° and groaned.
But we did not slack off, kept pitching rocks from this side
    and that.
Then we heard this awful exhortation: 320
"Pylades, we're about to die. Let's die brilliantly!
Draw your sword and follow me!"
At sight of their swords we fled back to the ravines
and as each one fled, others pressed forward   325
bombarding the strangers.
And if these were pressed back

the ones retreating pelted them with stones.
Yet here was the amazing thing:
so many hands throwing—not one hit the victims!
Anyway, in the end, however unheroically, we won the day.　　330
Surrounded them and knocked° the swords from their hands
　　with rocks.
They sank to their knees exhausted.
We brought them to our king,
who took one look and dispatched them here
for you to wash and sacrifice.　　335

Lady, these strangers are exactly the sort of victims
you should pray for.
Execute them and Greece will really be paying you back
for your own murder,
paying the price for that slaughter at Aulis.

CHORUS LEADER
Amazing story!—whoever this man is　　340
who's come from Hellas to the Hostile Sea.

IPHIGENIA
Okay, off you go.
Bring the strangers back with you
and we'll attend to sacred duties here.

(Exit Herdsman to the side.)

O my poor breaking heart,
once you were kind and compassionate to strangers;　　345
you always spared them a kindred tear when they were
　　Greeks.
But dreams have ensavaged me.
Whoever you are, you'll find me ill-disposed.　　350
This is the truth, it's clear to me, ladies:
our own bad luck does not make us benevolent
toward those who are worse off.
And the thing is,
no breeze of Zeus has ever come here,

no ship brought Helen through the Clashing Rocks   355
with her Menelaus
to pay back what they did to me—
they murdered me!—
to make an Aulis here for that Aulis there
where the Danaans laid their hands on me
as if I were a sacrificial calf
and my own father was the sacrificing priest!   360
I cannot forget those evils!
How many times did I fling my hands at his face crying,
"Father, you marry me to degradation!
While you're killing me here   365
my mother and her women in Argos
are singing wedding songs!
Our house fills with music of pipes
as I die at your hands!
Achilles, it seems, was Hades' son, not Peleus'—
you gave me him as a husband   370
and steered me into a wedding of blood.
It was just a filthy trick!"

And I did not lift my little brother in my arms—
who now is dead!
I did not kiss my sister; no, I
kept my face in veils for I was blushing—
I believed I was going to Peleus' house   375
and put off many an embrace till later,
thinking I'd come back to Argos again.
Poor Orestes—
if you are dead, what a fine patrimony you forfeit!
As for the sophistry of the goddess, I condemn it.   380
She who drives from her altar
anyone who touches blood or childbirth or corpses,
who calls them polluted,
this same goddess revels in human sacrifice!
Impossible the wife of Zeus is mother to such folly!   385

Nor do I credit that story of Tantalus' banquet—
how the gods happily digested a meal of his son.
The people here are murderous themselves,
this is my opinion,
so they ascribe base behavior to their deity.   390
No god is evil, I do not believe it.

CHORUS [*singing*]

STROPHE A

Deep deep blue roads of ocean
where the gadfly out of Argos
crossed the Hostile Sea°   395
from Asia to Europe,
who are these men who left behind the clear Eurotas
green with reeds   400
or the holy streams of Dirce
to come to this implacable country
where the altars and temples of Zeus' daughter   405
are doused with human blood?

ANTISTROPHE A

Did they sail to the double beat of pinewood oars
with ocean billows beneath them°
and an ocean breeze at their back   410
all for greed, for riches to bring home?
Don't fall in love with hope—it can be insatiable.°   415
Men lug rich cargo with them
as they roam strange cities and seas,
all suffering the same delusion.
Some people understand measure;   420
others can't think straight about wealth.

STROPHE B

How did they pass the Clashing Rocks
or the restless shores of Phineus
or the sea-swept coast of Amphitrite   425
where the fifty daughters of Nereus° dance in a circle and sing?
How did they go

racing the waves
with swelling sail
and hissing oar,   430
under southerly breeze
or western wind,
to the land where birds throng the White Shore   435
and Achilles
has his fair running ground
by the edge of the Hostile Sea?

ANTISTROPHE B

I pray along with my lady's prayers
that Helen might leave Troy and come here   440
to die at my lady's hands
with her throat cut   445
and a circle of bloody dew on her hair.
Helen ought to pay!
And how glad I would be
to hear some Greek traveler say
my miserable slavery is at an end.   450
Even in dreams°
how I long to go to my homeland
and share in the happiness there.   455

(Enter Orestes and Pylades from the side escorted by Taurian guards.)

[chanting]
But look, here come the two of them with their hands tied,
fresh victims for the goddess.
That herdsman wasn't lying.
Silence, women.
Choice Greek offerings are at hand.   460
Lady, if you are pleased with these civic rituals,
accept the sacrifice
which our own law calls unholy.   465

IPHIGENIA
So be it.

First I must take care that all arrangements for the goddess
   are correct.
Untie the strangers' hands.
They are sacred and should not be bound.
Now go in and prepare what is needed and proper for our
   task.   470

                    (*Exit the Taurian guards into the temple.*)

Ah pity.
Who is the mother who bore you,
the father, the sister—have you a sister?
Robbed of two young men like you
she will be brotherless now.   475
Who can know if his luck will lead in this direction?
Gods' plans are all invisible,
no one knows anything clear.
And luck seduces us sideways to stupidity.

Where did you come from, you poor strangers?
Surely you sailed a long way to get here.   480
And you'll stay a long time underground,
far from home.

ORESTES

Why do you lament these things and vex yourself
over troubles of ours—woman, whoever you are?
It doesn't make sense to me that someone bent on killing
wants to cancel the dread of death with pity.   485
Nor for a man near death with no hope of escape
to pity himself:
he makes one evil into two—
shows himself foolish and dies anyhow.
Let luck go its way.
Sing no dirges for us.   490
We know about the sacrifices here; we understand this.

IPHIGENIA

My first question is, which of you is Pylades?

ORESTES

If it please you, this man is Pylades.

IPHIGENIA

From what city of Greece?   495

ORESTES

What good will it do you to know this, woman?

IPHIGENIA

Are you two brothers, from one mother?

ORESTES

Brothers in love. We are not related.

IPHIGENIA

What sort of name did your father give you?

ORESTES

By rights I should be called Unlucky.   500

IPHIGENIA

Tell that to Fortune, it wasn't my question.

ORESTES

My body, not my name, is what you plan to sacrifice.

IPHIGENIA

Why begrudge this? You think you're so important?

ORESTES

If I die nameless I am spared mockery.

IPHIGENIA

You won't tell me your city either?   505

ORESTES

How will it profit me? I'm about to die.

IPHIGENIA

Then what prevents you granting it as a favor?

ORESTES

Glorious Argos is the home I claim.

IPHIGENIA

By the gods! Stranger, were you really born there?

ORESTES

In Mycenae, once a splendid city. 510

IPHIGENIA

You are surely welcome here if you've come from Argos.° 515

ORESTES

Not by my reckoning! Maybe yours. 516

IPHIGENIA

Did you leave your home as an exile, or why? 511

ORESTES

A kind of exile. Willing and unwilling at once.

IPHIGENIA

Will you tell me something I want to know?

ORESTES

Well, it might distract me from my problems. 514

IPHIGENIA

You've heard of Troy, whose fame is everywhere? 517

ORESTES

How I wish I never had, even in dreams!

IPHIGENIA

They say it is gone, wiped out by war.

ORESTES

That is the case, no idle rumor. 520

IPHIGENIA

And Helen's gone home to Menelaus' house?

ORESTES

She has. And her going brought harm to one of mine.

IPHIGENIA

Where is she now? She owes a debt to me as well.

ORESTES

She lives in Sparta with her former husband.

IPHIGENIA

O object of hatred—for the Greeks, not just me!   525

ORESTES

Yes, I've felt the effect of her marriages too.

IPHIGENIA

And the homecoming of the Achaeans was as reported?

ORESTES

Your questions certainly encompass everything!

IPHIGENIA

I want to make the most of you before you die.

ORESTES

Ask away then, I'll answer your pleasure.   530

IPHIGENIA

Did a prophet named Calchas come back from Troy?

ORESTES

He's dead according to the story at Mycenae.

IPHIGENIA

Excellent! What of Laertes' son, Odysseus?

ORESTES

Not reached home yet, but he lives, they say.

IPHIGENIA

May he perish and never reach home!   535

ORESTES

Don't bother cursing him: his whole life has gone wrong.

IPHIGENIA

And Achilles is alive?

ORESTES

No he is not. A futile marriage he made at Aulis.

IPHIGENIA

A travesty of marriage, so people say who suffered it.

ORESTES

Who are you? Your questions about Greece are strangely apt.   540

IPHIGENIA

I came from there. Was lost as a child.

ORESTES

Naturally you long for news of it, woman.

IPHIGENIA

And what of the general, the one they called "blessedly
happy"?

ORESTES

I'm not aware of one I'd call "blessedly happy."

IPHIGENIA

A son of Atreus, King Agamemnon, was so called.   545

ORESTES

I don't know. Change the subject.

IPHIGENIA

By the gods, no! Answer my question, stranger!

ORESTES

The poor man is dead. And took another with him.

IPHIGENIA

Dead? How? Oh no! Oh no!

ORESTES

Why do you groan? What's he to you?   550

IPHIGENIA

I groan for the great good fortune he once had.

ORESTES

Hideously he perished, murdered by his wife.

IPHIGENIA

Oh there are tears in this—for the killer and the killed!

ORESTES

Stop now. No more questions.

IPHIGENIA

Just this one: is the poor man's wife alive?   555

ORESTES

No, she is not. Her own son killed her.

IPHIGENIA

O house confounded! What did he want?

ORESTES

To avenge his father dead at her hands.

IPHIGENIA

Pity! He did well then, to carry out so righteous a wrong.

ORESTES

Righteous or not, he wins no grace from gods.   560

IPHIGENIA

And Agamemnon left another child at home?

ORESTES

One daughter, Electra.

IPHIGENIA

Is there not some tale of another daughter, sacrificed?

ORESTES

None except she's dead and looks no more upon the daylight.

IPHIGENIA

Pity that girl, pity the father who slew her.   565

ORESTES

Her death: a thankless gift to an evil woman.

IPHIGENIA

And the dead king's son, he lives in Argos?

ORESTES

He lives in misery, nowhere and everywhere.

IPHIGENIA

False dream, farewell, you were nothing after all!

ORESTES

Nor are the so-called wise gods   570
any more reliable than winged dreams.°

CHORUS LEADER

I feel a sudden sorrow! What of my mother and father—   576
are they alive? Dead? Who can say?

IPHIGENIA

Listen:
I've got a plan, beneficial for you, beneficial for me as well.
And things tend to succeed, do they not,
when one plan is pleasing to all.°   580
Would you be willing, if I saved your life,
to take a message to my loved ones at Argos—
a writing tablet inscribed for me by a captive
who took pity on me once?   585
(He didn't blame me for his murder,
but rather the law of the gods.)°
I've had no one to send the letter with till now.   590
But you are not ill-disposed to me, it seems,
and you know Mycenae, you know the people I mean.
So keep your life and go there—you'll win no mean reward—
salvation in return for a little letter.
And this man here, since the city requires it,   595
can be the goddess' victim, apart from you.

ORESTES

    Fine plan, strange lady, except one thing.
    This man's death would be a terrible weight on me.
    I am captain of this ship of catastrophes;
    he sails with me as friend to my need.   600
    How unjust for me to win favor myself,
    to slip out of harm's way and let him die.
    So how about this.
    Give the letter to him
    (he'll take it to Argos, your purpose is served)
    and let whoever wants to kill me kill me.   605
    It is utterly base to save oneself
    by sabotaging one's friends.
    This man is my friend and that's that.
    No less than myself I want him to look upon the daylight.

IPHIGENIA

    O excellent spirit! What nobility you were born from,
    what a true friend you are.   610
    I wish my one surviving brother were a man such as you—
    yes I do have a brother,
    though I never see him.
    But since it is your wish, we'll send this fellow
    off with the letter
    and you shall die.   615
    A profound desire for this seems to possess you.

ORESTES

    Who will sacrifice me and bear the horror?

IPHIGENIA

    I have this duty from the goddess.

ORESTES

    Not an enviable duty, girl, nor a lucky one.

IPHIGENIA

    But necessary and I must honor it.   620

ORESTES

You, a female, kill men with a sword?

IPHIGENIA

No, but I'll sprinkle sacred water around your head.

ORESTES

Who does the actual slaughtering if I may ask?

IPHIGENIA

Inside this temple are men who have that function.

ORESTES

And what sort of grave will receive me?   625

IPHIGENIA

Sacred fire inside then a wide chasm in the rock.

ORESTES

Ah! How I wish my sister's hand could lay me out!

IPHIGENIA

That is a pointless prayer, you poor man, whoever you are.
She lives far from this barbarian country.
But still, since you're Argive   630
I'll not stint from giving you all I can possibly give.
I shall lay much ornament on your grave,
anoint° your body with yellow oil,
and throw on your fire
the flowery brightness of yellow bees.   635

Well, I go. I shall bring you the letter from the temple.
And so you won't hate me—

                                             (To the servants.)

no fetters.
Guard them here unbound.

I wonder if my news will come as a shock at Argos—
whomever I send to—   640

a shock of incredible joy—
to hear that the one they thought dead is alive!

(Exit into the temple.).

CHORUS [*singing*]   *(To Orestes.)*
   I cry for you,
   for your end marked out,
   the bloody rain of lustral water.   645

ORESTES [*speaking*]
   This needs no pity, strangers, be joyful.

CHORUS [*singing*]   *(To Pylades.)*
   But you, young man blessed in fortune,
   we honor you, soon to set foot on your native land.

PYLADES [*speaking*]
   There is nothing blessed about friends going to their death.   650

CHORUS [*singing*]
   O grim journey!
   O death near at hand!
   What sorrow! My heart hesitates   655
   which to lament.

ORESTES
   Pylades, by the gods, do you have the same feeling as I?

PYLADES
   I can't say.

ORESTES
   Who is this young girl?
   How very Greek her questions   660
   about the troubles at Troy, the Achaean returns,
   wise Calchas and his birds, the name of Achilles!
   What pity she showed when she asked after poor
      Agamemnon,
   his wife, his children.   665

She comes from there, this strange woman, she is Argive by
     birth
or she would not be sending this letter;
she'd not be probing these matters in general
as if she had some share in the fortunes of Argos.

PYLADES

You're a little ahead of me—still, I agree
except for one thing: 670
this royal family's woes are familiar
to any reasonably alert person.
Still I have another worry.

ORESTES

Share it. You'll think better.

PYLADES

It would be shameful for me to go on living
while you do not.
I sailed with you and I must die with you.   675
Coward and criminal they'll call me in Argos
and in the folded hills of Phocis
if I come home alone.
Most men (most men are malicious) will assume
I betrayed you to get home safely.
Or even murdered you,
plotted your death to get your power,
now that your kingship is tottering   680
and I'm married to your sister who stands to inherit it.
I feel both fear and shame.
For me to breathe my last with you is absolutely the right
     thing.
To be killed and set on a pyre with you, yes.   685
I am your friend. I dread the blame.

ORESTES

Don't say that. My hardships are mine to bear.

Where trouble is single I won't make it double.
You say base and shameful—it's the same for me
if I make you share in my suffering and cause your death.   690
In fact for me personally it's no catastrophe,
faring as I do at the hands of gods,
to cease from life.
But you, you're successful and your house is sound,
not sick. Mine is defiled, unlucky.
Now if you live on and get sons from my sister   695
whom I gave you to wife,
my name will survive,
my ancestral house will not vanish childless.

No, you go. Live your life. Keep my father's house.
And when you reach Greece and horse-breeding Argos,   700
by your right hand I lay this charge upon you:
build me a burial mound and set a monument on it.
Have my sister give tears to the tomb and locks of her hair.
Report how I perished by the hand of some Argive woman
at an altar, consecrated to death.   705
Do not forsake my sister ever,
though you see the marriage, the house, desolate.

And now, farewell. You are the dearest friend I found.
You hunted with me, you shared my upbringing,
you bore with my pains and despairs.   710
Prophetic Apollo betrayed me and lied to me.
He used a trick to drive me as far away from Greece as I
    could go
because he was ashamed of his own former prophecies.
I gave myself to him—trusting his words
I murdered my mother. Now I die in turn!   715

PYLADES
Yes, you will have your burial.
And your sister's bed I'll not betray, O my poor comrade,

for I shall hold you a more beloved friend
dead than living.
Still, the oracle of god has not yet destroyed you
though you stand right next to death.   720
And it is the case, you know it is the case,
that extraordinary misfortune
can call forth extraordinary reversals:
all it takes is luck.

(Enter Iphigenia from the temple.)

ORESTES

Silence! The word of Phoebus is no help to me at all.
And here comes the woman from the house.

IPHIGENIA   *(To servants.)*

Go, go in, get everything ready   725
for the men in charge of the sacrifice.

(To Orestes and Pylades.)

Here is the letter, strangers, folded up tight.
And here's what I want in addition:
no man is the same when he's under stress
as when he regains confidence.   730
My fear is, no sooner he quits this land—
the one who takes my news to Argos—
than he consigns the letter to oblivion.

ORESTES

So what do you want?

IPHIGENIA

Let him swear an oath he will carry this letter   735
to my people in Argos, the ones I choose.

ORESTES

And you'll give such an oath in return?

IPHIGENIA

    To do or say what?

ORESTES

    To let him go alive from this barbarous land.

IPHIGENIA

    That sounds fair. How else could he carry the message?   740

ORESTES

    And the king will go along with this?

IPHIGENIA

    Yes, I'll persuade him. And put the man on board a boat
       myself.

ORESTES   *(To Pylades.)*

    Go ahead, swear.

                                     (To Iphigenia.)

    And you dictate an oath that's properly pious.

IPHIGENIA

    Say "I will give this letter to your loved ones."

PYLADES

    I will give this letter to your loved ones.   745

IPHIGENIA

    And I will send you safe past the dark-blue rocks.

PYLADES

    To which god will you swear this oath?

IPHIGENIA

    Artemis, in whose house I hold office.

PYLADES

    And I by the king of heaven, sublime Zeus.

IPHIGENIA

And if you forsake your oath and do me wrong?   750

PYLADES

May I never reach home. And you, if you do not save me?

IPHIGENIA

May I never set foot in Argos so long as I live.

PYLADES

Oh but listen, here's a point we've overlooked.

IPHIGENIA

Share it.

PYLADES

Grant me this exception: should something happen to the
   ship   755
so the letter is lost in the waves along with the cargo
and I can save only my skin,
the oath is off.

IPHIGENIA

Here's what I'll do (let's maximize our options):
I'll tell you everything written in the folds of the letter.   760
You can repeat it to my loved ones.
That way we're safe. If you get the letter there intact
it can tell its own tale silently.
But if the writing disappears in the sea
you'll save my words by saving yourself.   765

PYLADES

A good plan for both of us.
Tell me who is to receive the letter
and what to say from you.

IPHIGENIA

Give the message to Orestes, son of Agamemnon:
"The one slaughtered at Aulis sends you word—   770

Iphigenia, who is alive
although at Argos they think otherwise."

ORESTES
Where is she? Come back from the dead?

IPHIGENIA   *(To Orestes.)*
You're looking at her.
Now stop interrupting.

                                             (To Pylades.)

Say "Bring me to Argos before I die, brother,
out of this barbarous land!   775
Free me from my official task
of slaughtering strangers for a goddess!"

ORESTES
What shall I say, Pylades? Where in the world are we?

IPHIGENIA
"Or I'll become a curse on your house, Orestes!"
(That name you'll learn from hearing it twice.)

ORESTES°
O gods!

IPHIGENIA
Why are you invoking gods amid my instructions?   780

ORESTES
No reason. Go on. My mind wandered.
I'm on the verge of some miracle—no more questions.

IPHIGENIA
Tell them Artemis rescued me
by putting a deer in my place,
which my father sacrificed
thinking his sharp knife was slicing into me.   785

The goddess settled me in this land.
That is my message
as written in the letter.

PYLADES

Oh these oaths are easy to swear
and what you swore was beautiful too!
I won't take long to fulfill my vow.

(To Orestes.)

Behold, I bring you this letter from your sister,   790
your sister, Orestes, right here.

ORESTES

And I do welcome it!
But I shall lay the writing aside
and take hold of a joy that is not just words!
O dearest beloved sister, I am stunned   795
but I embrace you with my disbelieving arms
in open joy! This news astounds me!

IPHIGENIA°

Stranger, you transgress! It defiles the servant of a goddess
to touch her inviolable robes.

ORESTES

O my sister, born like me from Agamemnon,   800
don't turn away! You're holding the brother you never
    thought to hold again.

IPHIGENIA

You my brother? Stop this talk! Argos is his territory, and
    Nauplia.

ORESTES

Poor woman, that's not where your brother is.   805

IPHIGENIA

But who is your mother—Tyndareus' daughter from Sparta?

ORESTES

Yes, and my father is grandson of Pelops.

IPHIGENIA

What are you saying? Have you any proof?

ORESTES

Yes. Ask me anything about our father's house.

IPHIGENIA

Shouldn't you go first?   810

ORESTES

Yes. First this, I heard it from Electra:
you know there was strife between Atreus and Thyestes?

IPHIGENIA

Yes, some quarrel about a golden lamb.

ORESTES

So you know you wove it into a fine piece of cloth?

IPHIGENIA

Oh dear one, you come very close to my own heart.   815

ORESTES

And you also wove one showing the sun turned back in its
course?

IPHIGENIA

I did, I wove this too, into a fine, fine cloth.

ORESTES

And the ritual bath you got from your mother at Aulis?

IPHIGENIA

Yes! There was no happy marriage to cancel that memory.

ORESTES

And what about sending your mother locks of your hair?   820

IPHIGENIA

They belonged on my grave, not my body.

ORESTES

Now I'll give you the proofs I've seen myself:
that ancient spear in our father's house—
the one Pelops wielded
the day he won Hippodameia at Pisa
and killed Oenomaus—   825
it's hidden in your old bedroom.

IPHIGENIA [*singing in this interchange with Orestes, who speaks in reply*]

O most beloved! Nothing else—you are my most beloved!
Far from our fatherland, far from Argos,°
but I have you, O my love.   830

ORESTES

And I have you,
though you were dead. So people thought.

IPHIGENIA

Tears and lamentation mixed with joy,
make your eyes wet, and mine.
That day I left you, left you behind, just an infant,
just a babe in the house.   835
O happiness greater than words!
O my soul, what can I say?
These things have gone far beyond amazement,
beyond language.   840

ORESTES

From now on I pray we are happy side by side.

IPHIGENIA

I cannot place the joy I feel, O my friends, O ladies,
yet I fear it'll take wing and fly from my hands to the sky!
O Cyclopean hearth, O fatherland,   845
O dear Mycenae,
I thank you for his life,

I thank you for his cherishing:
you've raised a light of salvation for our house,
this brother of mine.

ORESTES

We are blest in our birth
but not in our contingencies, O my sister.   850
Ours is no lucky life.

IPHIGENIA

I realized that
the day my poor father laid his sword on my throat.

ORESTES

O poor love, I was not there but I can see it.   855

IPHIGENIA

There was no wedding song, brother,
when I was so treacherously led to the bed of Achilles.
By the altar instead were tears and lamentations.   860
Alas! I say alas, for the ritual waters poured out there.

ORESTES

Alas! I say it too, for the deed my father dared.

IPHIGENIA

He was no father to me.
Still, things do look different now   865
through some godsent stroke of luck.°   867

ORESTES

Pitiful woman, suppose you had murdered your brother!   866

IPHIGENIA

Pitiful indeed, and I did have it in me to do that!
Dread things I dared, dread things, brother.   870
You barely escaped an unholy death at my hands.
And how will it end?°   875
What chance will arise?

What means will I find to send you away
from violent death in a foreign land
to our home in Argos
before the bloody sword descends on you? 880
O my soul, this is your task: find the way.
Should it be on land, not by sea but on foot? 885
But death is nearby in the form of savage tribes
and impassable roads.
Yet surely that narrow passage through the dark-blue rocks
makes a long journey. 890
Ah, I feel desperate.
What god or mortal or miracle° 895
will find a way where there is no way
and show two lone offspring of Atreus
their exit from evils?

CHORUS LEADER
This is all quite astounding, beyond words — 900
and I saw it with my own eyes!

PYLADES
When loved ones meet, Orestes, it's natural for them
to fall into one another's arms
but now you must leave off emotion and confront the issue:
how shall we win the glorious name of salvation 905
and escape this barbaric land?
It's the mark of a wise man to accept his luck for what it is,°
seize the moment, maximize his happiness.

ORESTES
Well said. And I think we have luck on our side here.
If someone acts resolute, the divine force is more effective
too. 910

IPHIGENIA
You'll not restrain or silence me until I learn
what fate befell Electra.
This matters a great deal to me.°

ORESTES

She is happily married to Pylades here. 915

IPHIGENIA

And where is he from? Whose son is he?

ORESTES

Strophius of Phocis is his father.

IPHIGENIA

So he's born of a daughter of Atreus—he is my kinsman?

ORESTES

Yes, cousin to you and sole true friend to me.

IPHIGENIA

He was not yet born when my father killed me? 920

ORESTES

No, Strophius was childless a long time.

IPHIGENIA

I greet you, husband of my sister.

ORESTES

And my savior too, not just our kinsman.

IPHIGENIA

But how did you nerve yourself for those horrific deeds
against our mother?

ORESTES

Let's not talk of it. I was avenging my father. 925

IPHIGENIA

What cause had she to kill her husband?

ORESTES

Let our mother be! It's an evil thing for you to hear.

IPHIGENIA

I am silent. But does Argos look to you now as its leader?

ORESTES
    Menelaus rules there. I am exiled from my land.

IPHIGENIA
    Surely our uncle did not take advantage of our faltering
        house?°   930

ORESTES
    No, fear of the Furies drove me away.   931

IPHIGENIA
    I understand: the goddesses haunted you for our mother's
        sake.   934

ORESTES
    To force their bloody bit onto my mouth.   935

IPHIGENIA
    Your fit of madness on the shore—was that their doing?   932

ORESTES
    Not the first time I've been a spectacle of suffering.   933

IPHIGENIA
    But why did you make your way here?   936

ORESTES
    On orders from Phoebus.

IPHIGENIA
    To do what? Are you permitted to say?

ORESTES
    Yes, I can say. Here's how my troubles began:
    after I undertook those dread deeds against our mother,
    which I pass over in silence,   940
    I was driven into exile with the Furies at my heels,
    first Delphi,
    then Athens, where Apollo sent me°
    to render justice to the goddesses whose names we do not
        name.

For there is a holy court there established once by Zeus   945
to cleanse Ares' hands of blood pollution.
At first when I arrived
none of my guest-friends was willing to receive me,
a man despised by gods as I am.
But some felt ashamed and gave me a table off by myself
although under the same roof.   950
They addressed no word to me so that
I might enjoy my food and drink apart from them.
Each filled his own jug with equal measure of wine
and took his pleasure.
Pretending not to notice, I challenged no one,   955
suffering in silence
and groaning deep in myself that I was a mother-killer.
(I hear the Athenians made a ritual of my misfortune
and still keep the custom of the Three-Quart Jug.)   960

Then I came to the Hill of Ares and stood trial,
I on one platform, the eldest Fury on the other.
We each said our piece about my mother's murder
and Phoebus saved me with his testimony.   965
Athena counted out the votes: half for me.
I left my own murder trial a victor.
So all the Furies who acceded to the judgment
settled in a holy shrine right near the court.
But the Furies who dissented from the law   970
began to drive me in an endless restless chase
until I came again to Phoebus' holy ground
and laid myself before his sanctuary.
I was starving myself
and I swore I would cut my life off and die there on the spot
if Phoebus did not save me—he had ruined me!   975
Then Phoebus shrieked out from his golden tripod
and sent me here to get the statue that fell from the sky.
I am to set it up in Athens.
Come,

help me accomplish the salvation set out for us.
If we can seize the statue of the goddess
my mad fits will end
and I'll sail you back to Mycenae on our well-oared boat.   980
O dearest beloved, O dear sister's head,
save your father's house, save me!
All is lost for me,
all is lost for the race of Pelops,   985
unless we get our hands on that heaven-dropped statue.

CHORUS LEADER
Some dread wrath of a god has boiled up
against the seed of Tantalus and drives it on through woes.

IPHIGENIA
Since before you came here, brother, I've had an intense
    desire
to be in Argos and set my eyes on you.   990
I want what you want: to release you from troubles
and restore our ailing ancestral home—
for I've no anger left for my killer.
That way I could withdraw my hand from your slaughter
and save our house.
But how to elude the goddess   995
and also the king (when he finds that empty base robbed of
    its statue)
this gives me pause.
How shall I escape death? What story can I come up with?
On the other hand, if our plan works,
you'll take the statue and me on board your fine ship   1000
and the risk dissolves.
Apart from this, I perish,
though you may accomplish your task and get away home.
Well, I do not shrink. Not even if I die to save you.
Because you know, when a man is lost from home   1005
they long for him. But a woman doesn't signify.

ORESTES

I will not be the murderer of you as well as my mother!
Her blood is enough. I'm your partner—I want
to share life and death with you equally.
I shall bring you home, provided I get there,   1010
or stay here and die by your side.
But listen—I wonder, if this were displeasing to Artemis
why would Loxias give me an oracle
to take her statue away to Athena's city
and look upon your face?   1015
On that calculation, I'm hopeful of achieving our return.

IPHIGENIA

Yes, how can we both avoid death and get what we want?
This is the weak point in our homecoming plan,
though the will is there.

ORESTES

Could we kill the king?   1020

IPHIGENIA

Horrific suggestion, for strangers to murder their host.

ORESTES

But if it will save you and me, worth risking.

IPHIGENIA

I couldn't do it, but I admire your energy.

ORESTES

What if you hid me in the temple here?

IPHIGENIA

Thinking to escape under cover of darkness?   1025

ORESTES

Yes—night belongs to thieves, daylight to truth.

IPHIGENIA

There are guards in the temple, we could not elude them.

ORESTES

Oh I give up, we're ruined. What way out is there?

IPHIGENIA

I think I have a new idea.

ORESTES

What? Share it, teach me.   1030

IPHIGENIA

I'll turn your troubles to use in a cunning way.

ORESTES

Women are awfully good at scheming.

IPHIGENIA

I'll declare you came from Argos a murderer of your mother.

ORESTES

Use my misery, if it profits you.

IPHIGENIA

We'll say it isn't permitted to sacrifice you to the goddess.   1035

ORESTES

On what grounds? Or can I guess?

IPHIGENIA

On the grounds you're impure. I'll be keeping the sacrifice
    holy.

ORESTES

So how is this better for capturing the statue?

IPHIGENIA

I shall propose to purify you in seawater.

ORESTES

But the statue we need is still in the temple.   1040

IPHIGENIA

And to wash that too. Because you touched it, I'll say.

ORESTES

Where will you go on the sea's wet shore?

IPHIGENIA

To where your ship is moored by its flaxen ropes.

ORESTES

Will you or someone else bring the statue in your hands?

IPHIGENIA

I myself. To touch it is holy for me alone.   1045

ORESTES

And Pylades here, what task will he have?

IPHIGENIA

He'll be said to share the same pollution as you.

ORESTES

You'll do this in secret from the king or not?

IPHIGENIA

I'll win him with words—no way to prevent him noticing.   1049
So you must take care, take very great care, of everything else.   1051

ORESTES

Well, our fine-oared ship is standing ready.°   1050

IPHIGENIA

And one last thing: these women must join in our deception.°   1052

ORESTES

Exhort them, then; find convincing arguments.
A woman has the power to stir pity.
And everything else might just work out perfectly!   1055

IPHIGENIA   (To the Chorus.)

Dearest friends, I look to you.
My fate is in your hands, whether it turn out well
or come to naught with me bereft of my homeland,
my beloved brother, my own dear sister.

Let this be the substance of my appeal: 1060
we are women, as a species devoted to one another,
staunch in defending our common interests.
Keep silence for us and support our attempt to escape.
A loyal tongue is a fine thing.
Look how one turn of fate encircles the three of us   1065
joined in love—to reach home or die.
And besides, if I survive you'll share my good luck,
I'll get you back safe to Greece. Come, I entreat you,
and you, by your right hand, your dear cheek,   1070
your loved ones at home,
by your mother, your father, your child if you have one°—
what do you say? Who says yes, who says no?
Speak out:
if you reject me I perish and my poor brother too.

CHORUS LEADER

Take heart, dear lady. Do but save yourself.   1075
All is silence on my side, as you request,
let great Zeus be witness!

IPHIGENIA

Bless your words and bless your fortunes!

(To Orestes and Pylades.)

Your task now is to enter the temple.
The king will be here any minute   1080
to investigate whether the strangers' sacrifice is done.
O goddess who saved me in the folds of Aulis
from a terrible murdering father's hand,
save me now too along with these men—
or else by your fault is the word of Loxias   1085
discredited among mortals.
Be gracious, depart this barbarous land,
go to Athens.
It is not right for you to dwell here
when you could have a city blessed and happy.

(*Exit Iphigenia, Orestes, and Pylades into the temple.*)

CHORUS [*singing*]

STROPHE A

Halcyon bird who
all along the rocky sea ridges   1090
sings that song of sorrow
understood by those who know
you always mourn your husband,
how like you I am!—
in my lament
a bird without wings,   1095
longing for Greek marketplaces,
for Artemis goddess of childbirth
who dwells on the Cynthian hill,
for the delicate palm
and the flourishing bay   1100
and the sacred silver olive shoot
so dear to Leto in her travail,
for the lake of circling waters
where a melodious swan
pays service to the Muses.   1105

ANTISTROPHE A

O streams of tears
that fell down my cheeks
the day the towers were toppled,
the day I was shipped off
by enemy oar and enemy spear.   1110
I was trafficked for gold
and got a barbarian home.
Here I serve the girl
who serves deer-killer Artemis—
Agamemnon's daughter,   1115
at an altar where no sheep die.
And I envy the man whose life is solid misery—
amid necessity

he does not grow exhausted
because he lives with it every day.
But happiness keeps shifting.   1120
To fall into evils after good fortune
makes a heavy life for a mortal.

STROPHE B

Now you, lady—an Argive ship
will carry you home
and the waxbound reed of mountain Pan   1125
will call out to the beat of the oars
while prophetic Apollo
singing along with his seven-stringed lyre
brings you safe
to the bright shore of Athens.   1130
But I,°
I will be left behind here
when you go your way on dashing oars
and the sails   1135
of your swift-running ship
are spread to the air.

ANTISTROPHE B

If only I could travel those blazing roads
that fiery Helios travels,
then right above my own chambers at home   1140
I would stop
my wings in midair.
If only I could take my place in the dances°
where once as a girl at fancy weddings   1145
I made my feet whirl
alongside my girlfriends—
we were rivals in grace,
in delicate ornaments
and eager to win the contest.
I decked myself in robes of rich design   1150
and let my hair hang down to shadow my cheeks.

(Enter Thoas from the side.)

THOAS

Where is the woman who keeps these gates,
the Greek? Has she consecrated the strangers already?
Are their bodies ablaze inside the shrine?   1155

(Enter Iphigenia from the temple bearing a statue.)

CHORUS

Here she is, king, she will answer you plainly.

THOAS

Ho there! daughter of Agamemnon!
Why are you hoisting this statue of the goddess off its base?

IPHIGENIA

Stop right there in the doorway, king.

THOAS

Is there something unusual happening in the temple,
Iphigenia?   1160

IPHIGENIA

I spit that away (a word to keep things holy).

THOAS

What are you hinting? Speak out plainly.

IPHIGENIA

The victims you've caught for me are not pure, king.

THOAS

What evidence do you have—or is this your own notion?

IPHIGENIA

The goddess' image turned its back.   1165

THOAS

All on its own or did an earthquake turn it?

IPHIGENIA

All on its own. It closed its own eyes too.

THOAS

For what reason? The pollution of the strangers?

IPHIGENIA

Exactly, yes. Dread deeds were done by them.

THOAS

They murdered some barbarian on the shore?   1170

IPHIGENIA

They were carrying bloodstains from home when they came
here.

THOAS

What bloodstains? I'm very curious.

IPHIGENIA

They cut down their mother with a common sword.

THOAS

Apollo! Not even a barbarian would dare that.

IPHIGENIA

They were pursued all through Greece.   1175

THOAS

So that's why you're bringing the statue out?

IPHIGENIA

Yes, out to the holy open air, away from bloodstains.

THOAS

And how did you discover the strangers' pollution?

IPHIGENIA

I interrogated them when the statue turned around.

THOAS

How perceptive! Greece raised you to be clever.   1180

IPHIGENIA

Besides, they set out a sweet bait for me.

THOAS

Tried to charm you with some news from Argos?

IPHIGENIA

That my only brother, Orestes, is faring well.

THOAS

So you would spare them, I guess, in joy at their news.

IPHIGENIA

And that my father is alive and prospering too.   1185

THOAS

Naturally you remained loyal to the goddess.

IPHIGENIA

Oh yes, I hate Greece utterly. Greece ruined me!

THOAS

Then what should we do about the strangers, tell me.

IPHIGENIA

We must honor the existing law.

THOAS

But aren't your lustrations and sword already at work?   1190

IPHIGENIA

I want to cleanse them first with purifying rituals.

THOAS

In fresh-flowing streams or water of the sea?

IPHIGENIA

The sea washes away all human evil.

THOAS

Yes, they'll be purer victims for your goddess surely.

IPHIGENIA

    And that might improve my lot too.   1195

THOAS

    Doesn't the sea wash up right here by the temple?

IPHIGENIA

    We need a deserted spot—we have other tasks to do.

THOAS

    Take them wherever you want. I've no desire to see forbidden
        things.

IPHIGENIA

    I must purify the goddess' statue as well.

THOAS

    Yes you must, if the matricides' pollution touched her.   1200

IPHIGENIA

    Why else would I have lifted her from her pedestal?

THOAS

    Your piety and forethought are impeccable.

IPHIGENIA

    Do you know what I'd like you to do?

THOAS

                      Tell me.

IPHIGENIA

    Tie the strangers up.

THOAS

                 But where could they escape to?

IPHIGENIA

    You can't trust anything Greek.

THOAS

                Servants, fetch ropes.   1205

IPHIGENIA
Let them bring the strangers out here . . .

THOAS
                                    So be it.

IPHIGENIA
. . . Covering their heads with robes.

THOAS
                        To keep off the gaze of the sun.

IPHIGENIA
Send some of your servants with me.

THOAS
                              These will attend you.

IPHIGENIA
And send someone to announce to the city . . .

THOAS
                                    What?

IPHIGENIA
. . . that they should all stay indoors.

THOAS
                        To avoid contact with blood?   1210

IPHIGENIA
Yes, such things do pollute.

THOAS   *(To servant.)*
                        You, go, make the announcement . . .

IPHIGENIA
. . . that no one come into their sight.

THOAS
                        How well you care for our city!

IPHIGENIA

And for the friends I have to protect.

THOAS

You mean me!

IPHIGENIA°

THOAS

No wonder our whole community admires you.

IPHIGENIA

You yourself stay here before the temple and . . .

THOAS

What shall I do?   1215

IPHIGENIA

. . . cleanse the chamber of the goddess with sulfur.

THOAS

So it's pure for your return.

IPHIGENIA

And when the strangers emerge . . .

THOAS

What should I do?

IPHIGENIA

. . . pull your robe in front of your eyes.

THOAS

So as not to look on a guilty man.°

IPHIGENIA

And if I seem to take too long . . .

THOAS

What limit do I set for this?

IPHIGENIA

. . . don't be surprised.

THOAS

Take your time, do the work
of the goddess properly.   1220

IPHIGENIA

May this purification go according to plan!

THOAS

I second this prayer!

(Enter Orestes and Pylades from the
temple escorted by Taurian guards.)

IPHIGENIA

Here come the strangers now out from the temple.
I see ornaments for the goddess and newborn lambs too—
I shall wash blood with blood to get rid of the defilement—
and blaze of torches and all the other purifications
I ordered for the men and the goddess.   1225
I call upon you citizens to keep your distance from this
    pollution—
anyone who keeps his hands pure as doorkeeper of a temple,
anyone about to enter a marriage,
anyone heavy with child:
keep back, step away, lest this uncleanness fall upon you.
O virgin queen, child of Zeus and Leto,   1230
if I succeed in washing the blood from these men
and performing the requisite sacrifice,
your dwelling will be purified
and we shall prosper.
As for the rest,
I do not say it but I make a sign
to the gods who know more
and to you, goddess.

(Exit Iphigenia, Orestes, and Pylades to the side,
escorted. Exit Thoas into the temple.)

CHORUS [*singing*]

A fine son is Leto's:
she bore him in the fruitful fields of Delos　　　　　　　1235
a god with golden hair.
He is a master of the lyre and loves
to sight an arrow straight along the bow.
She left the place of her travail and carried her child
from the sheer sea cliffs　　　　　　　　　　　　　　1240
to the mother of rushing waters
who dances for Dionysus
on top of Mount Parnassus
where a wine-dark speckle-backed snake,　　　　　　　1245
monster of earth,
glittered from the shade of a laurel tree,
guarding the oracle.°
You were still an infant
bouncing in your mother's arms,　　　　　　　　　　1250
O Phoebus,
when you killed it
and mounted your holy oracle:
now you sit on the golden tripod,
in the place that tells no lies,
dispensing to mortals god-spoken oracles
from your sanctuary　　　　　　　　　　　　　　　1255
in the middle room of the world
beside Castalia's streams.

But when he had removed Themis, child of Gaia,°　　1260
from her holy oracle,
Earth concocted dream phantoms of night
who revealed things to the cities of men—
how it all began, what came next, the future—　　　1265
as they slept in their beds wrapped in dark.
So Gaia, jealous for her daughter,

robbed Phoebus of his oracular office.
He went straight to Olympus
on his swift feet,   1270
wrapped his child hands around Zeus' throne
and begged
that the earth goddess' anger be banished
from his Pythian home.
Zeus laughed
to see his son so quick and greedy
for solid gold oblations.   1275
With a shake of his head he stopped the night voices—
stole from mortals those truths that take shape in the night—
gave back his honors to Loxias   1280
and upon those mortals
who throng his throne
he bestowed
trust
in the singing of the god's word.

(Enter Messenger from the side.)

MESSENGER
O temple guards and keepers of the altars,
where is Thoas, king of this land, to be found?   1285
Throw open these bolted doors and call him out.

CHORUS LEADER
Why, if I may ask?

MESSENGER
The two young men are clean gone.
By the schemes of Agamemnon's daughter   1290
they're fleeing this land and taking
the holy image on board their Greek ship.

CHORUS LEADER
That's incredible. But the king you want is not here,
he rushed out of the temple.

MESSENGER

    Where to? He needs to know what's happening.   1295

CHORUS LEADER

    No idea. Run after him, find him
    and tell him your news.

MESSENGER

    See how treacherous is the female species!
    You too have some share in these goings-on, don't you?

CHORUS LEADER

    You're mad. What would escaping foreigners have to do
        with us?   1300
    And shouldn't you be hastening off to the palace gates?

MESSENGER

    Not until an interpreter tells me
    whether the king is inside or not.
    Hey, you inside, undo these bolts!
    And tell your master I'm here at the door   1305
    with a boatload of bad news.

                    (Enter Thoas from the temple.)

THOAS

    Who's making this racket at the house of the goddess,
    banging doors, interrupting us inside?

MESSENGER

    These women lied to me,° kept trying to drive me away,
    said you were out. But you were here all the time!   1310

THOAS

    Why? What did they think to gain?

MESSENGER

    I'll explain that later. Listen to what's happening right now.
    The young girl who was in charge of the altar here, Iphigenia,
    has fled the land along with the strangers   1315
    and the holy statue. The purification was a trick.

THOAS

What do you mean? What lucky breeze did she catch?

MESSENGER

She is saving Orestes. Surprise for you!

THOAS

Who? You mean the boy who is son of Tyndareus' daughter?

MESSENGER

Yes, and the one who'd been dedicated by the goddess for this
    altar.   1320

THOAS

That's amazing! What more can I say?

MESSENGER

Don't fuss about it, just hear me out:
when you've thoroughly listened and pondered,
plan a way to track those foreigners down.

THOAS

You're right, go ahead. They have no short voyage   1325
ahead of them if they think to escape my spear.

MESSENGER

Well, when we came to the shore of the sea
where Orestes' ship was secretly anchored,
holding on to those strangers' ropes as you bid us,
Agamemnon's daughter signaled us to stand back   1330
saying she was kindling forbidden fire
and performing special purificatory rites.
Then she took their ropes in her own hands
and walked behind them.
Now this was suspicious
but your servants went along with it, my lord.   1335
After a while, to give the impression she was doing
    something,
she let out an ululation and started chanting

barbarian songs, as if she were
some kind of priest cleansing blood pollution.

And when we'd been sitting a long time on the ground
it struck us that once they were set free   1340
the strangers might kill her and make their escape.
We sat in silence, afraid to look at things forbidden.
But finally the same conclusion came to us all,
to go where they were, forbidden or not.
There we saw the Greek ship   1345
fitted with oars that spread out like wings
and fifty sailors holding their oars on the pins
and the young men—loose from their bonds—
standing on the stern.
Some sailors were holding the bow with poles,   1350
some were fastening the anchor to its supports,
others hastened to lower ladders from the stern
into the sea for the foreign woman.

Well, we lost restraint now that we'd seen her treachery.
Laying hold of the foreign woman and the stern ropes   1355
we began pulling the steering oars out of their sockets.
Words went back and forth:
"What's your explanation—making off from our land
with statues and priestesses?
Who are you, whose son are you, trafficking this woman
    away?"   1360
The other replied:
"I am Orestes, for your information,
brother of this woman, son of Agamemnon.
And the woman I'm transporting is my own sister, lost from
    home."
Still we held on to her,
trying to force her to come along with us to you.   1365
That's how I got these terrible knocks on the jaw!
They had no iron to hand, nor had we,
but fists were pummeling

and kicks were landing from both young men at once
onto our ribs and livers— 1370
the pain was intense, our limbs grew exhausted.
Covered in awful marks we fled to the cliff,
bloody and wounded on heads and faces.
Then taking a stand on the hill we fought more cautiously 1375
and pelted with rocks.
But archers stationed on the ship's stern
were hindering us with arrows and keeping us back.
Meanwhile
a monstrous wave had run the ship aground
and the girl° was afraid to wet her foot 1380
so Orestes took her on his left shoulder,
stepped into the sea and leapt onto the ladder,
setting his sister down on the well-benched ship
along with that thing that fell from the sky—
the image of Zeus' daughter.
And from midship there came a shout: 1385
"You band of sailors from the land of Greece,
take your oars, make the sea white with foam.
We have the prize for which we sailed through
the hostile passage of the Clashing Rocks."

They roared out a glad shout 1390
and struck the salt sea. And so long as the ship
was within the harbor it kept advancing
but as it crossed the mouth
it went under
the deluge of a violent wave.
For a terrible wind came up suddenly
and was thrusting the ship backward.
They persevered, kicking against the wave, 1395
but a back-rushing surf was driving the ship to land.
Then Agamemnon's daughter stood up and prayed:
"O daughter of Leto,
send me, your priestess, safe

back to Greece from this barbarian land
and forgive my thievery.   1400
You surely love your brother, goddess.
Know that I too love my kin."

The sailors seconded the girl's prayer with a paean
and at a command put their bare shoulders to the oars.   1405
But the boat was coming more and more toward the rocks.
Then one of our men leapt into the sea on foot,
another tried to catch the woven ropes,
and I was sent straight here to you
to let you know what's happening over there, king.   1410
Go then, bring bonds and ropes with you.
For unless the rising sea turns quiet again
there is no hope of salvation for these strangers.
Reverend Poseidon, ruler of the ocean and
watcher over Troy, is hostile to Pelops' family.   1415
And now it seems he will deliver Agamemnon's son
into your hands—yours and your citizens'—
along with his guilty sister—she who forgot
the sacrifice at Aulis and betrayed her own goddess.

CHORUS LEADER

O poor Iphigenia, you will die with your brother
now you've fallen again into the tyrant's hands.

THOAS

I address you all, people of this barbarian land.
Come, throw reins on your horses and race along the shore
to welcome the wreck of the Greek ship,   1425
and while some of you hurry to hunt down these impious
    men
with the help of the goddess,
others will drag swift vessels into the water
so we can take them by sea and ride them down on land,
then throw them off a steep rock   1430
or skewer their bodies on stakes!

And you women who collaborated in these plots,
I'll punish you later at my leisure.
Right now I'm busy, can't linger.

(Enter Athena above the temple.)

ATHENA

Where oh where are you off to on this hot pursuit, King
   Thoas? 1435
Hear what I, Athena, have to say!
Stop your hunting; don't launch the full flood of your men.
It was fated by Loxias' oracles for Orestes to come here
fleeing the anger of Furies,
to transport his sister back home to Argos 1440
and bring the holy image to my land,
so to find rest from his toils.
This is the word I have for you.
As for Orestes,
whom you expect to catch and kill on the tossing sea,
Poseidon is even now, as a favor to me,
smoothing the waves for his oar to traverse. 1445
Orestes (you do hear my divine voice
though you are not present),
heed my instructions.
Take the image and your sister and go.
When you reach god-built Athens, 1450
there is a place near the far edge of Attica,
close by the hills of Carystus,
a holy place called Halae by my people.
There build a temple and set down the statue.
Call it "Tauric" after the Taurian land
and the ordeals you survived,
roaming up and down Greece goaded by Furies. 1455
People in future will hymn her as Artemis Tauropolus.
And you must establish this custom:
when they celebrate her festival
let them hold a sword at a man's throat and draw blood, 1460

in payment for your sacrifice—so to mark its sanctity
and let the goddess keep her honors.
Now you, Iphigenia,
must continue to hold the keys of this goddess
in the holy meadows of Brauron.
There you will die and be buried
and they will make an offering to you
of finewoven robes left behind in their homes   1465
by women who die in childbirth.
As for these women of Greece—I command you
to send them from this country
as reward for their righteousness.°
I rescued you once already, Orestes,
on the Hill of Ares when I judged the votes equal.   1470
This too shall become customary:
whoever gets equal votes will win his case.
Go then, child of Agamemnon,
bring your sister out of this land.
And you, Thoas, calm your rage.

THOAS

Queen Athena, that man is not in his right mind   1475
who hears gods' words and disobeys.
I harbor no rage against Orestes for departing with the
    image,
nor against his sister.
Is there any good in fighting powerful gods?
Let them go to your land and take the goddess' statue,   1480
let them enshrine it there with all success.
I will also send these women to blessed Greece
as you enjoin me.
And I will no longer raise my spear,
nor my ship's oars,
against the strangers,
since this is your will, goddess.   1485

ATHENA

I commend you.

Necessity governs both you and the gods.

Go, winds, convey the son of Agamemnon to Athens.

I shall accompany the voyage

to keep my sister's sacred image safe.

(Exit Athena.)

THOAS [chanting]

Go on your way rejoicing in good fortune,°   1490

blessed by salvation.

CHORUS [chanting]

O holy among immortals and mortals,

Pallas Athena,

we will do as you bid.

Surely delightful and unexpected   1495

is this utterance I hear.

O great holy Victory,°

may you uphold my life

and not cease to crown me with crowns.

(Exit all.)

ELECTRA

EURIPIDES
Translated by Emily Townsend Vermeule

INTRODUCTION TO EURIPIDES' ELECTRA

Euripides' *Electra* was probably written and produced around 420 BCE. Sophocles dealt with exactly the same material in his own *Electra*, which has also survived but cannot be dated precisely; scholars are divided about which of the two plays came first. Both of these plays cover the same material that was contained in Aeschylus' *Libation Bearers*, the second play of his *Oresteia*.

Euripides adopts in some respects a more "realistic" approach to the story of Orestes' and Electra's revenge on their mother than Aeschylus had done. How could this murder, how would it in fact, have been done? The recognition scene of Aeschylus is deliberately mocked, and a more plausible one substituted. The difficulty of entering the palace and eluding the palace guards is avoided by setting the scene in the country, near the frontiers of the kingdom. There Electra lives, married to a humble but honorable farmer, her husband in name only. There Orestes, a nervous homicide, lurks, concealing his identity until he is recognized. There Aegisthus and Clytemnestra, separately, are set upon and killed. The villains are not, it seems, quite so bad as they have been made out to be. A courteous Aegisthus is hewn down while he is being hospitable to strangers. Clytemnestra is more vain and weak than malignant; she is not happy over her career, and she is murdered while performing an act of kindness. Orestes and Electra lack heroic stature. Castor and Polydeuces, the "Dioscuri" or heavenly twins (Clytemnestra's brothers), appear aloft at the end as *deus ex machina*. They accept what has been done, but disapprove of Apollo's command and of the deed of matricide.

ELE<TRA

Characters FARMER, married to Electra
ELECTRA, daughter of Agamemnon
and Clytemnestra
ORESTES, son of Agamemnon and
Clytemnestra
PYLADES, a friend of Orestes (nonspeaking)
CHORUS of Argive peasant women
OLD MAN
MESSENGER, a servant of Orestes
CLYTEMNESTRA, widow of Agamemnon,
mother of Electra and Orestes
CASTOR and POLYDEUCES (the Dioscuri),
Clytemnestra's brothers

Scene: In front of the Farmer's cottage in the countryside near Argos; before the house stands an altar to Apollo.

FARMER

Argos, old bright floor of the world,° Inachus' pouring
tides—King Agamemnon once on a thousand ships
hoisted the war god here and sailed across to Troy.
He killed the monarch of the land of Ilium,
Priam; he sacked the glorious city of Dardanus;   5
he came home to Argos here and high on the towering
   shrines
nailed up the massive loot of Barbary for the gods.
So, over there he did well. But in his own house

he died in ambush planned for him by his own wife
Clytemnestra and by her lover Aegisthus' hand.   10
    He lost the ancient scepter of Tantalus; he is dead.
Thyestes' son Aegisthus walks king in the land
and keeps the dead man's wife for himself, Tyndareus' child.
As for the children he left home when he sailed to Troy,
his son Orestes and his flowering girl Electra,   15
Orestes almost died under Aegisthus' fist,
but his father's ancient servant snatched the boy away,
gave him to Strophius to bring up in the land of Phocis.
Electra kept on waiting within her father's house.
But when the burning season of young ripeness took her,   20
then the great princes of the land of Greece came begging
her bridal. Aegisthus was afraid—afraid her son
if noble in blood would punish Agamemnon's death.
He held her in the house sundered from every love.
Yet, even guarded so, she filled his nights with fear   25
lest she in secret to some prince might still bear sons;
he laid his plans to kill her. But her mother, though
savage in soul, then saved her from Aegisthus' hand.
The lady had excuse for murdering her husband
but flinched from killing a child, afraid of the world's ill will.   30
So then Aegisthus framed a new design. He swore
to any man who captured Agamemnon's son
running in exile and murdered him, a price of gold.
Electra—he gave her to me as a gift, to hold
her as my wife.
                        Now, I was born of Mycenaean   35
family, on this ground I have nothing to be ashamed of,
in breeding I shine bright enough. But in my fortune
I rank as a pauper, which blots out all decent blood.
He gave her to me, a weak man, to weaken his own fear,
for if a man of high position had taken her   40
he might have roused awake the sleeping Agamemnon's
blood—justice might have knocked at Aegisthus' door.
I have not touched her and the love god Cypris knows it:

I never shamed the girl in bed, she is still virgin.
I would feel ugly taking the daughter of a wealthy man   45
and violating her. I was not bred to such an honor.
And poor laboring Orestes, my brother-in-law in name—
I suffer his grief, I think his thoughts, if he came home
to Argos and saw his sister so unlucky in her wedding.

    Whoever says that I am a born fool to keep   50
a young girl in my house and never touch her body,
I say he measures wisdom by a crooked line
of morals. He should know he's as great a fool as I.

(Enter Electra from the house, carrying a water jar on her head.)

ELECTRA

    O night, black night, whose breast nurses the golden stars,
I wander through your darkness, head lifted to bear   55
this pot I carry to the sources of the river—
I do not need to, I chose this slavery myself
to demonstrate to the gods Aegisthus' outrageousness—
and cry my pain to Father in the great bright air.
For my own mother, she, Tyndareus' deadly daughter,   60
has thrown me out like dirt from the house, to her husband's
    joy,
and while she breeds new children in Aegisthus' bed
has made me and Orestes mere appendages to the house.

FARMER

    Now why, unhappy girl, must you for my sake wrestle
such heavy work though you were raised in comfort?   65
Although I tell you often to stop, you just refuse.

ELECTRA

    I think you equal to the gods in kindliness:
for you've never taken advantage of me though I'm in
    trouble.
It's great fortune for people to find a kind physician
of suffering, which I have found in finding you.   70
Indeed without your bidding I should make your labor

as light as I have strength for; you will bear it better
if I claim some share with you in the work. Outdoors
you have enough to do; my place is in the house,
to keep it tidy. When a man comes in from work   75
it is nice to find his hearthplace looking swept and clean.

FARMER

Well, if your heart is set on helping, go. The spring
is not so distant from the house. At light of dawn
I will put the cows to pasture and start planting the fields.
A lazy man may rustle gods upon his tongue   80
but never makes a living if he will not work.

> (*Exit Farmer and Electra to the side. Enter Orestes and
> Pylades from the other side, with attendants.*)

ORESTES

Pylades, I consider you the first of men
in loyalty and love to me, my host and friend.
You only of my friends gave honor and respect
to me, Orestes, suffering as I suffer from Aegisthus.   85
He killed my father—he and my destructive mother.
I come from secret converse with the holy god
to this outpost of Argos—no one knows I am here—
to counterchange my father's death for death to his killers.
During the night just passed I found my father's tomb,   90
gave him my tears in gift and sheared my hair in mourning,
and sprinkled ceremonial sheep's blood on the fire,
holding these rites concealed from the tyrants who rule here.
     I will not set my foot inside the city walls.
I chose this gatepost of the land deliberately,   95
compacting a double purpose. First, if any lookout
should recognize me I can run for foreign soil;
second, to find my sister. For they say she married
and, tamed to domestic love, lives here no longer virgin.
I want to be with her and take her as my partner   100
in killing, and learn more about things inside the city.

And now, since lady dawn is lifting her white face,
let's come away from the path on which we have been
    treading.
Perhaps a field-bound farmer or some serving woman
will meet us on the road, and we can ask discreetly   105
whether my sister lives anywhere in this place.

Quick now! I see some sort of serving girl approach
with a jar of fountain water on her close-cropped head—
it looks heavy for her. Let's sit here, let us listen
to the slave girl. Pylades, perhaps at last we shall hear   110
the news we hoped for when we crossed into this land.

(*They hide behind the altar. Enter Electra from the side.*)

ELECTRA [*singing*]

STROPHE A

Quicken the foot's rush—time has struck—O
walk now, walk now weeping aloud,

O for my grief!

I was bred Agamemnon's child,   115
formed in the flesh of Clytemnestra,
    Tyndareus' hellish daughter,
Argos' people have named me true:

wretched Electra.

Cry, cry for my toil and pain,   120
    cry for the hatred of living.
Father who in the halls of death
lie hacked by your wife and Aegisthus, O
Agamemnon!

MESODE A

Come, waken the mourning again,   125
rouse up for me the sweetness of tears.

ANTISTROPHE A

Quicken the foot's rush—time has struck—
walk now, walk now weeping aloud,
    O for my grief!

In what city and in what house, O   130
brother of grief, do you wander in exile?°
    You left me locked in the cursed
palace chambers for doom to strike
    your sister in sorrow.
Come, loose me from miseries, come   135
    save me, pitiful me—O Zeus,
Zeus!—to help avenge our father's hate-spilled blood,
steering your exiled foot to land
        in Argos.

Set this vessel down from my head, O   140
take it, while I lift music of mourning
    by night to my father.
Father, the maenad song of death°
    I cry you among the dead
beneath the earth, the words I pour   145
    day after day unending
as I move, ripping my throat with sharp
nails, fists pounding my shorn
    head for your dying.

Ai, ai, strike my head!   150
I, like the swan of echoing song
in descant note at the water's edge
who calls to its father so dearly loved
but dead now in the hidden net
of twisted meshes, mourn you thus   155
    in agony dying, father,

body steeped in the final bath,
rest most pitiful, sleep of death.
O for my grief!
Bitter the axe and bitter the gash,   160

bitter the road you walked°
　from Troy straight to their plotted net—
　　　your lady did not receive you
　with victor's ribbons or flowers to crown you,
　but with double-edged steel she made you
　savage sport for Aegisthus, and won　　　　　　　　　165
　　　　　herself a shifty lover.

　　　　(Enter the Chorus of Argive peasant women from the side.)

CHORUS [singing in a lyric interchange with Electra, who continues to
sing]
　　　　　　　　STROPHE
　Princess, daughter of Agamemnon,
　we have come to your country dwelling,
　　　　　　　Electra, to see you.
　There came, came a man
　　　　　　　bred on the milk of the hills,
　a Mycenaean mountaineer　　　　　　　　　　　　170
　who gave me word that two days from now
　the Argives proclaim at large
　a holy feast, when all the maidens
　will pass in procession up to the temple of Hera.

ELECTRA
　Dear friends, not for festivities,　　　　　　　　　175
　not for twisted bracelets of gold
　　　does my heart take wing in delight.
　I am too sad, I cannot stand
　　　in choral joy with the maidens of Argos
　or beat the tune with my whirling foot;　　　　　　180
　　　rather with tears by night
　and tears by day I fill my soul
　　　shaking in grief and fear.
　Look! Think! Would my filthy hair
　and robe all torn into slavish rags　　　　　　　　185
　do public honor to Agamemnon's

> daughter, the princess?
> Honor to Troy which will never forget
>   my conquering father?

CHORUS

<subheading>ANTISTROPHE</subheading>

> Great, great is the goddess. Come,   190
> I will lend you a dress to wear,
>   thick-woven of wool,
> and gold—be gracious, accept—
>   gold for holiday glitter.
> Do you think your tears and refusing
> honor to the gods will ever hurt   195
> your haters? Not by sounding lament
> but only by prayer and reverent love
> for the gods, my child, will you have gentler days.

ELECTRA

> Gods? Not one god has heard
> my helpless cry or watched of old   200
>   over my murdered father.
> Mourn again for the wasted dead,
>   mourn for the living outlaw
> somewhere prisoned in foreign lands
> passing from one laborer's hearth to the next   205
>   though born of a glorious sire.
> And I! I in a peasant's hut
> waste my life like melting wax,
> exiled and barred from my father's home
>   to a scarred mountain field,   210
> while my mother rolls in her bloody bed
>   and plays at love with another man.

CHORUS LEADER [*speaking*]
Yes, like Helen, your mother's sister—charged and found
guilty of massive pain by Greece and by your house.

(*Orestes and Pylades appear from behind the altar.*)

[196] EURIPIDES

ELECTRA [*now speaking*]
Oh, oh! women, I break off my death-bound cry.   215
Look! there are strangers here close to the house who crouch
huddled beside the altar and rise up in ambush.
Run, you take the path, and I into the house
with one swift rush can still escape these criminals.

ORESTES
Poor girl, stand still, and fear not. I would never hurt you.   220

ELECTRA
Phoebus Apollo, help! I kneel to you. Do not kill me.

ORESTES
I hope I shall kill others hated more than you.

ELECTRA
Go away; don't touch. You have no right to touch my body.

ORESTES
There is no person I could touch with greater right.

ELECTRA
Why were you hiding, sword in hand, so near my house?   225

ORESTES
Stand still and listen. You will agree I have rights here.

ELECTRA
I stand here utterly in your power. You are stronger.

ORESTES
I have come to bring you a spoken message from your
    brother.

ELECTRA
Dearest of strangers, is he alive or is he dead?

ORESTES
Alive. I wish to give you all the good news first.   230

ELECTRA
God bless your days, as you deserve for such sweet words.

ORESTES

I share your gift with you that we may both be blessed.

ELECTRA

Where is he now, attempting to bear unbearable exile?

ORESTES

He is wrecked, and is included in no city's laws.

ELECTRA

Tell me, he is not poor? not hungry for daily bread?   235

ORESTES

He has bread, yet he has the exile's constant hunger.

ELECTRA

You came to bring a message—what are his words for me?

ORESTES

"Are you alive? And if you are, what is your life?"

ELECTRA

I think you see me. First, my body wasted and dry.

ORESTES

Yes, sadness has wasted you so greatly I could weep.   240

ELECTRA

Next, my head razor-cropped like a victim of the Scythians.

ORESTES

Your brother's life and father's death both bite at your heart.

ELECTRA

Alas, there's nothing else that I love more than them.

ORESTES

You grieve me. Whom do you think your brother loves
but you?

ELECTRA

He is not here. He loves me, but he is not here.   245

ORESTES

Why do you live in a place like this, so far from town?

ELECTRA

Because I married, stranger—a wedding much like death.

ORESTES

Bad news for your brother. Your husband is a Mycenaean?

ELECTRA

But not the man my father would have wished me to marry.

ORESTES

Tell me. I am listening, I can say it to your brother.   250

ELECTRA

This is his house. I live quite isolated here.

ORESTES

A ditchdigger, a cowherd would look well living here.

ELECTRA

He is a poor man but well born, and he respects me.

ORESTES

Respects? What does your husband understand by "respect"?

ELECTRA

He has never been violent or touched me in my bed.   255

ORESTES

A vow of chastity? or he finds you unattractive?

ELECTRA

He finds it attractive not to insult my royal blood.

ORESTES

How could he not be pleased at marrying so well?

ELECTRA

He judges the man who gave me had no right to, stranger.

ORESTES

I see—afraid Orestes might avenge your honor.   260

ELECTRA

Afraid of that, yes—he is also decent by nature.

ORESTES

Ah.
You paint one of nature's gentlemen. We must treat him well.

ELECTRA

We will, if my absent brother ever gets home again.

ORESTES

Your mother took the wedding calmly, I suppose?

ELECTRA

Women save all their love for their men, not for their
children.   265

ORESTES

What was in Aegisthus' mind, to insult you so?

ELECTRA

He hoped that I, so wedded, would have worthless sons.

ORESTES

Too weak for undertaking blood-revenge on him?

ELECTRA

That was his hope. I hope to make him pay for it.

ORESTES

This husband of your mother's—does he know you are
virgin?   270

ELECTRA

No, he knows nothing. We have played our parts in silence.

ORESTES

These women listening as we talk are friends of yours?

ELECTRA

Good enough friends to keep what we say well concealed.

ORESTES

How should Orestes play his part, if he comes to Argos?

ELECTRA

If he comes? Ugly talk. The time has long been ripe.   275

ORESTES

Say he comes; still how could he kill his father's killers?

ELECTRA

By being just as daring as once his enemies were.°

ORESTES

To kill your mother with his help—could you do that?

ELECTRA

Yes, with the very same axe that cut Father to ruin.

ORESTES

May I tell him what you say and how determined you are?   280

ELECTRA

Tell him how gladly I would die in Mother's blood.

ORESTES

O, I wish Orestes could stand here and listen.

ELECTRA

Yet if I saw him I should hardly know him, sir.

ORESTES

No wonder. You were both very young when you were parted.

ELECTRA

I have only one friend who might still know his face.   285

ORESTES

The man who saved him once from death, as the story goes?

ELECTRA

Yes, very old now—he was my father's tutor.

ORESTES

When your father died did his body find some burial?

ELECTRA

He found what he found. He was thrown on the dirt
  outdoors.

ORESTES

I cannot bear it. What have you said? Even a stranger's   290
pain bites strangely deep and hurts us when we hear it.
Tell me the rest, and with new knowledge I will bring
Orestes your tale, so harsh to hear but so imperative
to be heard. Uneducated men are pitiless,
but we who are educated pity much. And we pay   295
a high price for being intelligent. Wisdom hurts.

CHORUS LEADER

The same excitement stirs my mind in this as his—
I live far from the city and I know its troubles
hardly at all. Now I would like to learn them too.

ELECTRA

I will tell if I must—and must tell you as my friend—   300
how my luck, and my father's, is too heavy to lift.
Since you have moved me to speak so, stranger, I must beg
that you will tell Orestes all my distress, and his.
First tell him how I am kept like a beast in stable rags,
my skin heavy with grease and dirt. Describe to him   305
this hut—my home, who used to live in the king's palace.
I weave my clothes myself and slavelike at the loom
must work or else walk naked through the world in nothing.
I fetch and carry water from the riverside,
I am deprived of holy festivals and dances,   310
I can't spend time with women since I am a girl,°
I can't spend time with Castor, who is close in blood
and was my suitor, before he rose to join the gods.
My mother in the glory of her Phrygian loot

sits on the throne, while circled at her feet the girls   315
of Asia stoop, whom Father won at the sack of Troy,
their clothes woven in snowy wool from Ida, pinned
with golden brooches, while the walls and floor are stained
still with my father's black and rotting blood. The man
who murdered him goes riding grand in Father's chariot,   320
with bloody hands and high delight lifting the staff
of office by which Father marshaled the Greek army.
The tomb of Agamemnon finds no honor yet,
never yet drenched with holy liquids or made green
in myrtle branches, barren of bright sacrifice.   325
But in his drunken fits, my mother's lover, brilliant
man, triumphant leaps and dances on the mound
and pelts my father's stone memorial with rocks
and dares to shout against us with his boldened tongue:
"Where is your son Orestes? When will that noble youth   330
come to protect your tomb?" Insults to an absent man.
    Kind stranger, as I ask you, tell him all these things.
For many call him home again— and I speak for them,
all of them, with my hands and tongue and grieving mind
and head, shaven in mourning; and his father calls too.   335
All will be shamed if he whose father captured Troy
cannot in single courage kill a single man,
although his strength is younger and his birth more noble.

CHORUS LEADER
Electra! I can see your husband on the road.
He has finished his field work and is coming home.   340

(The Farmer enters from the side.)

FARMER
Hey there! Who are these strangers standing at our gates?
What is the errand that could bring them to our distant
courtyard? Are they demanding something from me? A nice
woman should never stand in gossip with young men.

ELECTRA

My dearest husband, do not come suspecting me.   345
You shall hear their story, the whole truth. They come
as messengers to me with tidings of Orestes.
Strangers, I ask you to forgive him what he said.

FARMER

What news? Is Orestes still alive in the bright light?

ELECTRA

So they have told me, and I do not doubt their words.   350

FARMER

Does he still remember his father's troubles, and yours?

ELECTRA

We hope so. But an exile is a helpless man.

FARMER

Then what is this message of his? What have they come to
tell?

ELECTRA

He sent them simply to see my troubles for themselves.

FARMER

What they don't see themselves I imagine you have told
them.   355

ELECTRA

They know it all. I took good care that they missed nothing.

FARMER

Why were our doors not opened to them long ago?
Come into the house, you will find entertainment
to answer your good news, such as my roof can offer.
Servants, pick up their baggage, bring it all indoors.   360
Come, no polite refusals. You are here as friends
most dear to me who meet you now. Though I am poor
in money, I think you will not find our manners poor.

ORESTES
  By the gods! Is this the man who helps you fake a marriage,
  the one who does not wish to cast shame on Orestes?   365

ELECTRA
This is the man they know as poor Electra's husband.

ORESTES
  Alas,
  we try to find good men and cannot recognize them
  when met, since all our human heritage runs mongrel.
  At times I have seen descendants of the noblest family
  quite worthless, while poor fathers had outstanding sons;   370
  inside the souls of wealthy men bleak famine lives
  while minds of stature struggle trapped in starving bodies.
    How then can man distinguish man, what test can he use?°
  The test of wealth? That measure means poverty of mind.
  Of poverty? The pauper owns one thing, the sickness   375
  of his condition, a compelling teacher of evil.
  By nerve in war? Yet who, when a spear is aimed right at
  his face, will stand to witness his companion's courage?
  We might as well just toss these matters to the winds.
    This fellow here is no great man among the Argives,   380
  not dignified by family in the eyes of the world—
  he is a face in the crowd, and yet I choose him champion.
  Can you not come to understand, you empty-minded,
  opinion-stuffed people, to judge a man by how
  he lives with others: manners are nobility's touchstone?   385
  Such men of manners can control our cities best,°
  and homes, but the wellborn sportsman, long on muscle, short
  on brains, is only good for a statue in the park—
  not even sterner in the shocks of war than weaker
  men, for courage is the gift of character.   390
    Now let us take whatever rest this house can give;
  this man here, Agamemnon's child, the absent man
  for whom I've come, deserves no less. We should go now

indoors, servants, inside the house, since a poor host
who's eager to entertain is better than a rich one.   395
I do praise and accept his most kind reception
but would have been more pleased if your brother on the
    crest
of fortune could have brought me into a fortunate house.
Perhaps he may still come; Apollo's oracles
are strong, though human prophecy is best ignored.   400

(Exit Orestes and Pylades into the house with their attendants.)

CHORUS LEADER
    Now more than ever in our lives, Electra, joy
    makes our hearts light and warm. Perhaps now fortune, first
    running such painful steps, will stand on firmer footing.

ELECTRA   *(To the farmer.)*
    You thoughtless man! You know quite well the house is bare;
    why take these strangers in? They are better born than you.   405

FARMER
    Why? Because if they are the gentlemen they seem,
    will they not be content with small things as with great?

ELECTRA
    Small is the word for you. Now the mistake is made,
    go quickly to my father's loved and ancient servant
    who by Tanaus river, where it cuts the land   410
    of Argos off from Spartan country, goes his rounds
    watching his flocks in distant exile from the town.
    Tell him these strangers have descended on me;° ask
    him to come and bring some food fit for distinguished
        guests.
    He will surely be happy; he will bless the gods   415
    when he hears the child he saved so long ago still lives.
    Besides, we cannot get help from the family house,
    from Mother—our news would fly to her on bitter wings,
    cruel as she is, if she should hear Orestes lives.

FARMER

    Well, if you wish it, I can pass your message on   420
    to the old man. But you get quick into the house
    and ready up what's there. A woman when she has to
    can always find some food to set a decent table.
    The house holds little, yet it is enough, I know,
    to keep these strangers full of food at least one day.   425

(Exit Electra into the house.)

    When things like this occur, my intellect reflects.
    I contemplate the mighty power found in money:
    money you can spend on guests; money you can pay the
      doctor
    when you get sick. But little difference does money make
    for our daily bread, and when a man has eaten that,   430
    the rich man and the poor one hold just the same amount.

(Exit the Farmer to the side.)

CHORUS [*singing*]

STROPHE A

O glorious ships that sailed across to Troy once
    moving on infinite wooden oars
    attending the circling chorus of Nereid dancers
where the dolphin delighting in the pipe-   435
    melody all about the sea-
    blue prows went plunging;
you led the goddess Thetis' son,
light-striding Achilles, on his way
with Agamemnon to Ilium's cliffs   440
    where Simois pours into the sea.

ANTISTROPHE A

The Nereids passed Euboea's headlands
    bringing the heavy shield of gold,
forged on Hephaestus' anvil, and golden armor.
Up Mount Pelion, up the jut   445

of Ossa's holy slopes on high,
   up the nymphs' spy-rocks
they hunted the aged horseman's hill
where he trained the boy as a dawn for Greece,
the son of Thetis, sea-bred and swift-   .   450
   footed for the sons of Atreus.

STROPHE B

Once I heard from a man out of Troy, known to the port
   in Nauplia close to Argos,
     of your brilliant shield, O goddess'
child, how in its circled space   455
these signs, scenes, were in blazon warning,
   terrors for Phrygia:
running in frieze on its massive rim,
Perseus lifting the severed head
of the Gorgon, cut at the neck;°   460
he walks on wings over the sea;
Hermes is with him, messenger of Zeus,
   great Maia's
child of the flocks and forests.

ANTISTROPHE B

Out of the shield's curved center glittered afar the high
   shining round of the sun   465
     driving with wingèd horses,
and the chorused stars of upper air—
Pleiades, Hyades—Hector eyed them,
   and swerved to flight.
Over the helmet of beaten gold   470
Sphinxes snatch in hooking nails
their prey trapped with song. On the hollow
greave, the lioness' fire breath
flares in her clawed track as she runs,
   staring
at the wind-borne foal of Peirene.   475

All along the blade of the deadly sword, hooves pounding,
horses leapt; black above their backs the dust blew.
But the lord of such spearmen
  you killed by lust of sex and sin   480
    of mind, daughter of Tyndareus.
For this the sons of heaven will send
you a judgment of death;° some far
day I shall still see your blood fall   485
red from your neck by the iron sword.

(*Enter the Old Man from the side, carrying provisions for a feast.*)

OLD MAN

Where is my young mistress and my lady queen,
the child of Agamemnon, whom I raised and loved?
How steep this house seems set to me, with rough approach,
as I grow old for climbing on these withered legs.   490
But when your friends call, you must come and drag along
and hump your spine till it snaps and bend your knees like
    pins.

(*Enter Electra from the house.*)

Why there she is—my daughter, look at you by the door!
I am here. I have brought you from my cropping sheep
a newborn lamb, a tender one, just pulled from the teat,   495
and flowers looped in garlands, cheese white from the churn,
and this stored treasure of the wine god, aged and fragrant—
not much of it, I know, but sweet, and very good
to pour into the cup with other, weaker wine.
Let someone take this all in to the guests indoors,   500
for I have cried a little and would like to dry
my face and eyes out here on my cloak—more holes than
    wool.

(*A servant does as instructed.*)

ELECTRA

    Old man, please tell me, why is your face so stained with
       tears?
    After so long has my grief stirred your thoughts again,
    or is it poor Orestes in his cheerless exile   505
    you mourn for, or my father, whom your two old hands
    once raised and helped without reward for self or loved
       ones?

OLD MAN

    Reward, no. Yet I could not stop myself, in this:
    for I came past his tomb, circling from the road,
    and fell to the earth there, weeping for him, alone,   510
    and opening this winesack intended for your guests
    I poured libation, and I wreathed the stone in myrtle.
    And there I saw on the burning-altar a black-fleeced
    sheep, throat cut and blood still warm in its dark stream,
    and curling locks of bright blond hair cut off in gift.   515
    I stopped, quiet, to wonder, child, what man had courage
    to visit at that tomb. It could not be an Argive.

      Is there a chance your brother has arrived in secret
    and paused to wonder at his father's shabby tomb?
    Look at the lock of hair, match it to your own head,   520
    see if it is not exactly twin to yours in color.
    Often a father's blood, running in separate veins,
    makes siblings' bodies almost mirrors in their form.

ELECTRA

    Old man, I always thought you were wiser than you sound
    if you really think my brother, who is brave and bold,   525
    would come to our land in hiding, frightened by Aegisthus!
    Besides, how could a lock of his hair match with mine?
    one from a man with rugged training in the ring
    and games, one combed and girlish? It is not possible.
    Besides, you could find many matching curls of many people 530
    not bred in the same house, old man, nor matched in blood.

OLD MAN

At least go set your foot in the print of his hunting boot
and see if it is not the same as yours, my child.

ELECTRA

But how could rocky ground possibly receive
the imprint of a foot? And if it could be traced,   535
it would not be the same for brother and for sister,
a man's foot and a girl's—of course his would be bigger.

OLD MAN

Is there no piece then, if your brother should come home,°
of weaving, that loom pattern by which you would know the
   cloth
you wove and I wrapped him in, to rescue him from death?   540

ELECTRA

You know quite well that when Orestes left for exile
I was still very small. And even if a child's hand
could weave, how could a grown man still wear those boy's
   clothes
unless his shirt and tunic lengthened with his body?
Some pitying stranger must have passed the tomb and cut   545
a mourning lock, or townsmen slipping past the lookouts.°

OLD MAN

Where are the strangers now? I want to look them over
and draw them out with conversation of your brother.

(Enter Orestes and Pylades from the house.)

ELECTRA

Here they come striding lightly from the cottage now.

OLD MAN

Well. They look highborn enough, but the coin may prove   550
false. Often a noble face hides filthy ways.
Nevertheless—

                    Greetings, strangers, I wish you well.

ORESTES

And greetings in return, old sir.

Electra, tell me,
to what friends of yours does this human antique belong?

ELECTRA

This is the man who raised and loved my father, sir.   555

ORESTES

What! the one who saved your brother once from death?

ELECTRA

Indeed he saved him—if indeed he still is safe.

ORESTES

Ah, so!
Why does he stare upon me like a man who squints
at the bright stamp on silver? Do I look like somebody?

ELECTRA

Perhaps he's just happy seeing someone of Orestes' age.   560

ORESTES

Dear Orestes. Why does he walk round me in circles?

ELECTRA

Stranger, I am astonished too as I look at him.

OLD MAN

Mistress, now pray. Daughter Electra, pray to the gods.

ELECTRA

For which of the things I have, or which that I don't have?

OLD MAN

For a treasure of love within your grasp, which god reveals.   565

ELECTRA

As you please; I pray the gods. Now, what was in your mind?

OLD MAN

Look now upon this man, my child—your dearest love.

ELECTRA

I have been looking long already; are you crazy?

OLD MAN

And am I crazy if my eyes have seen your brother?

ELECTRA

What have you said, old man? What hopeless impossible
    word?   570

OLD MAN

I said I see Orestes—here—Agamemnon's son.

ELECTRA

How? What sign do you see? What can I know and trust?

OLD MAN

The scar above his eye where once he slipped and drew
blood as he helped you chase a fawn in your father's court.

ELECTRA

I see the mark of a fall, but I cannot believe you.   575

OLD MAN

How long will you stand, hold back from his arms and love?

ELECTRA

I will not any longer, for my heart has trust
in the token you show.
                      O Brother so delayed by time,
I hold you against hope . . .

ORESTES

                          And I hold you at last.

ELECTRA

. . . and never thought I'd see you.

ORESTES

                          I too abandoned hope.   580

ELECTRA

And are you he?

ORESTES

                              I am, your sole defender and friend.
Now if I catch the prey for which I cast my net!°
I'm confident. Or never believe in the gods' power
again if evil can still triumph over good.

CHORUS [*singing*]

You have come, you have come, our slow, bright day,   585
    you have shone, you have shown a beacon-
lit hope for the state, who fled of old
your father's palace, doomed and pained,
    drifting in exile.
Now god, some god restores us strong   590
    to triumph, my dear.
Lift high your hands, lift high your voice, raise
prayers to the gods, that in fortune, fortune
your brother may march straight to the city's heart.   595

ORESTES

Enough. I find sweet pleasure in embrace and welcome,
but let us give ourselves over to pleasure later.
Old man, you came on the crest of opportunity—
tell me what I must do to punish Father's killer
and Mother too who lives in foul adultery.   600
Have I in Argos any strong measure of friends
or am I bankrupt in backing as I am in fortune?
Whom shall I look to? Shall it be by day or night?
What hunting track will lead me toward my enemies?

OLD MAN

My son, you lost your friends when luck deserted you.   605
That would indeed be luck met on the road for you,
someone to share both good and evil without change.
But you from root to leaf-top have been robbed of friends
while, leaving, you left them without all hope. Hear me:
in your own hand and in your fortune you hold all,   610
to capture back your city, home, and patrimony.

ORESTES

But what should we be doing now to reach our goal?

OLD MAN

Kill him. Kill Thyestes' son. And kill your mother.

ORESTES

Such the triumphal crown I came for, yet—how reach it?

OLD MAN

Not inside the city even if you were willing.   615

ORESTES

Is he so strongly fenced by bodyguards and spears?

OLD MAN

You know it. The man's afraid of you and cannot sleep.

ORESTES

Let that go, then. Tell me another way, old man.

OLD MAN

Yes—you shall hear, for something came to me just now.

ORESTES

I hope your plan and my reaction are equally good.   620

OLD MAN

I saw Aegisthus as I hauled my way up here.

ORESTES

Good, that sounds hopeful. Where did you happen on him?

OLD MAN

Close, down in the meadows where his horses graze.

ORESTES

What was he doing? Out of despair I see new light.

OLD MAN

Offering a banquet to the goddess nymphs, I think.   625

ORESTES

To keep his children safe? Or for one not yet born?

OLD MAN

I know only that he was preparing to kill a bull.

ORESTES

How many men were with him? Simply alone with servants?

OLD MAN

No citizens were there; a handful of household servants.

ORESTES

No one who might still recognize my face, old man?   630

OLD MAN

They are his private servants and they have never seen you.°

ORESTES

And would they, if we conquered, be, ah—kindly disposed?

OLD MAN

That is characteristic of slaves, and luck for you.

ORESTES

How would you suggest my getting close to him?

OLD MAN

Walk past where he will see you as he sacrifices.   635

ORESTES

He has his fields, I gather, right beside the road?

OLD MAN

And when he sees you he will ask you to join the feast.

ORESTES

He shall find a bitter banquet-fellow, if god wills.

OLD MAN

What happens next—you play it as the dice may fall.

ORESTES

Well spoken. The woman who gave me birth is—where?   640

OLD MAN

In Argos. She will join him for the feast tonight.

ORESTES

But why did she—my mother—not start out with him?

OLD MAN

The gossip of the crowd disturbs her. She held back.

ORESTES

Of course. She feels the city's disapproving looks.

OLD MAN

That's how it is. Everyone hates a promiscuous wife.   645

ORESTES

Then how can I kill them both at the same time and place?

ELECTRA

I will be the one to manage my mother's killing.

ORESTES

Good—then fortune will arrange that business well.

ELECTRA

Let our single friend here help the two of us.

OLD MAN

It shall be done. What death have you decided for her?   650

ELECTRA

Old uncle, you must go to Clytemnestra; tell her°
that I am kept in bed after bearing a son.

OLD MAN

Some time ago? Or has your baby just arrived?

ELECTRA

Ten days ago, which days I have kept ritually clean.

OLD MAN

And how will this achieve the murder of your mother?   655

ELECTRA

She will come, of course, when she hears about the birth.

OLD MAN

Why? Do you think she cares so deeply for you, child?

ELECTRA

Yes—and she will weep about the boy's low breeding.

OLD MAN

Perhaps. Return now to the goal of your design.

ELECTRA

She will come; she will be killed. All that is clear.   660

OLD MAN

I see—she comes and walks directly in your door.

ELECTRA

From there she need go only a short way down to Hades.

OLD MAN

I will gladly die too, when I have seen her die.

ELECTRA

But first, old man, you ought to guide Orestes now.

OLD MAN

Where Aegisthus holds his sacrifices to the gods?   665

ELECTRA

Then go see my mother, tell her all about me.

OLD MAN

I'll speak so well she'll think it is Electra speaking.

ELECTRA   (To Orestes.)

Your task is ready. You have drawn first chance at killing.

ORESTES

Well, I will go if anyone will show me where.

OLD MAN

I will escort you on your way with greatest joy.   670

ORESTES°

O Zeus of our Fathers, now be Router of Foes,
have pity on us, for our days are piteous.

OLD MAN

Pity them truly—children sprung of your own blood.

ELECTRA

O Hera, holy mistress of Mycenae's altars,
grant us the victory if our claim to victory is just.   675

OLD MAN

Grant them at last avenging justice for their father.

ORESTES

And you, O Father, dwelling wronged beneath the earth . . .

ELECTRA

. . . and Earth, ruler below, to whom I stretch my hands . . .

OLD MAN

. . . protect, protect these children here, so dearly loved.

ORESTES

Come now and bring as army all the dead below . . .   680

ELECTRA

. . . who stood beside you at Troy with the havoc of their
     spears . . .

OLD MAN

. . . all who hate the godless guilty criminals.

ORESTES

Did you hear us, wretched victim of our mother?°

OLD MAN

All, your father hears all, I know. Time now to march.

ELECTRA

I call to you again and say: "Aegisthus dies!"°   685
And if, Orestes, in your struggle you should die,

I too am dead, let them no longer say I live,
for I will stab myself with a two-edged sword.

I will go in and make our dwelling fit for the outcome:
then if a message of good fortune comes from you   690
the whole house shall ring out in triumph. If you die
triumph will shift to desolation. This is my word.

ORESTES

I understand you.

ELECTRA

                    Make yourself fit man for the hour.
You, my women, with your voices scream a fire-
signal of shouting in this trial. I shall stand guard,   695
a sword raised ready for the issue in my hand.
If I'm defeated, I shall never grant to those
I hate the right to violate my living flesh.

                              (*Exit Orestes, the Old Man, and Pylades to*
                                    the side, Electra into the house.)

CHORUS [*singing*]

                    STROPHE A

The ancient tale is told
    in Argos
still—how a magic lamb   700
from its gentle mother on the hills
Pan stole, Pan of the wild
beasts, kind watcher, Pan
who breathes sweet music to his jointed reed.
He brought it to show the gold   705
curls of its wool. On the stone
steps a standing herald called:
"To the square, to the square, you men
of Mycenae! Come, run, behold
    a strange and lovely thing   710
for our blessed kings." Swiftly the chorus in dance
    beat out honor to Atreus' house.

The altars spread their wings
    of hammered
gold, fire gleamed in the town
like the moon on Argos' stones   715
of sacrifice, lotus pipes
tended the Muses, lilting
ripples of tune. The dance swelled in desire
tense for the lamb of gold—
whose? Quick, Thyestes' trick:
seducing in the dark of sleep   720
Atreus' wife, he brought
the strange lamb home, his own.
    Back to the square he calls
all to know how he holds the golden creature,
    fleece and horn, in his own house.   725

That hour—that hour Zeus
changed the stars on their blazing course,
utterly turned the splendid sun,
turned the white face of the dawn   730
so the sun drives west over heaven's spine
    in glowing god-lit fire.
The watery weight of cloud moved north,
the cracked waste of Egyptian Ammon
dried up, died, never knowing dew,   735
robbed of the beautiful rain that drops from Zeus.

Thus it is always told.
I myself am won only to slight belief
that the sun would swerve or change his gold
countenance of fire, moved in pain   740
and sorrow at sin in the mortal world,
    to judge or punish humans.
Yet terrible myths are useful,

they call men to the worship of the gods—
whom you forgot when you killed your husband,   745
sister of glorious brothers.

                                   (A cry is heard from offstage.)

Listen, listen.
Friends, did you hear a shout? Or did anxiety
trick me? A shout deep-rolling like the thunder of Zeus?

                                   (Another cry.)

Again it comes! The rising wind is charged with news.
Mistress, come out! Electra, leave the house!   750

                                   (Enter Electra from the house.)

ELECTRA
Dear friends, what is it? How do we stand now in our trial?

CHORUS
I only know one thing: I heard a voice of death.

ELECTRA
I heard it too. It was far off. But I too heard it.

CHORUS
It comes from a great distance, yet it is quite clear.

ELECTRA
Is it an Argive groaning there—or is it our friends?   755

CHORUS
I cannot tell; the note of clamoring is slurred.

ELECTRA
So you announce my death by sword. Why am I slow?

CHORUS
Lady, hold back until you learn the outcome clearly.

ELECTRA
Not possible. We are beaten. Where are the messengers?

CHORUS

They will come soon. To kill a king is not quick or light.   760

(Enter a Messenger, one of Orestes' servants, from the side.)

MESSENGER

Hail maidens of Mycenae, glorious in triumph!
Orestes is victor! I proclaim it to all who love him.
The murderer of Agamemnon lies on the earth
crumpled in blood, Aegisthus. Let us thank the gods.

ELECTRA

Who are you? Why should I think your message is the truth?   765

MESSENGER

You do not know you're looking on your brother's servant?

ELECTRA

Dearest of servants! Out of fear I held my eyes
shaded from recognition. Now indeed I know you.
What is your news? My father's hated murderer dead?

MESSENGER

Dead, dead. I say it twice if that is what you wish.   770

ELECTRA

O gods! O Justice watching the world, you have come at last.
How did he die? What style of death did Orestes choose,
to kill Thyestes' son? Give me the details.

MESSENGER

When we rose from your cottage and walked down the hill
we came across a beaten double wagon-track,   775
and there we found the new commander of Mycenae.
He happened to be walking in the water-meadow,
picking young green shoots of myrtle for his hair.
He saw us and called out: "You are most welcome, strangers.
Who are you? Have you traveled far? Where is your home?"   780
Orestes answered, "We are Thessalians on our way
toward Alpheus' valley where we shall sacrifice to Zeus

of Olympia." When Aegisthus heard, he called again,
"Now you must stop among us as our guests and share
our feast. I am at the moment slaughtering a bull   785
for the nymphs. Tomorrow morning you shall rise at dawn
and get there just as soon. Come with me to the house"—
while he was still talking he took us by the hand
and led us off the road—"I will take no refusal."
When we were in the house he gave his men commands: 790
"Quick, someone fill a bowl of water for the strangers
so their hands will be clean near the lustrations at the altar."
But Orestes interrupted: "We are clean enough.
We washed ourselves just now in the clear river water.
If strangers may join citizens in sacrifice,   795
we are here, Aegisthus. We shall not refuse you, prince."
      So this is what they said in public conversation.
Now the king's bodyguard laid down their spears
and sprang all hands to working.
Some brought the lustral bowl, and others baskets of grain,   800
some laid and lit the fire or around the hearth
set up the sacred ewers—the whole roof rang with sound.
Your mother's lover took the barley in his hands
and cast it on the altar as he said these words:
"Nymphs of the Rocks, may I kill many bulls for you,   805
and my wife, Tyndareus' child, who is at home.
Guard us in present fortune, ruin our enemies."
(Meaning you and Orestes.) But my master prayed
the utter reverse, keeping his words below his breath,
to take his dynastic place again. Aegisthus raised   810
the narrow knife from the basket, cut the calf's front lock,
with his right hand dedicated it to the holy fire,
and, as his servants hoisted the beast upon their shoulders,
slashed its throat.
                     Now he turns to your brother and says,
"One of your great Thessalian talents, as you boast,   815
is to be a man of two skills: disjointing bulls

and taming horses. Stranger, take the iron knife,
show us how true Thessalian reputation runs."
Orestes seized the beautifully tempered Dorian blade,
loosened his brooch, flung his fine cloak back from his
    shoulders,   820
chose Pylades as his assistant in the work,
and made the men stand off. Holding the calf by its foot,
he laid the white flesh bare by pulling with his hand.
He stripped the hide off whole, more quickly than a runner
racing could double down and back the hippodrome course, 825
and opened the soft belly. Aegisthus scooped the prophetic
portions up in his hands and looked.

                              The liver lobe
was missing. But the portal vein and gall sac showed
disaster coming at him even as he looked.
His face darkened, drew down. My master watched and
    asked,   830
"What puts you out of heart?" "Stranger, I am afraid.
Some ambush is at my door.° There is a man I hate,
the son of Agamemnon, an enemy to my house."
He answered, "You can scarcely fear a fugitive's
tricks when you control the state? So we can feast   835
on sacrificial flesh, will someone bring a chopper—
Phthian, not Dorian—and let me split this breastbone?"
He took it and struck. Aegisthus heaped the soft parts, then
sorted them out. But while his head was bent above them,
your brother stretched up, balanced on the balls of his feet, 840
and smashed a blow to his spine. The vertebrae of his back
broke. Head down, his whole body convulsed, he gasped
to breathe, writhed with a high scream, and died in his blood.

    The servingmen who saw it leaped straight to their spears,
an army for two men to face. And yet with courage   845
they stood, faced them, shook their javelins, engaged—
Pylades and Orestes, who cried, "I have not come
in wrath against this city nor against my servants.

I have only paid my father's killer back in blood.
I am the much-suffering Orestes—do not kill me, men   850
who helped my father's house of old."

                                            They, when they heard
his words, lowered their spears, and he was recognized
by some old man who used to serve the family.
Swiftly they crowned your brother's head with flower
    wreaths,
shouting aloud in joy and triumph. He comes to you   855
bringing something to show you—not the Gorgon's head,
only Aegisthus whom you loathe, who was in debt
for blood and found the paying bitter at his death.

                                              (Exit to the side.)

CHORUS [*singing*]

                   STROPHE
Come, lift your foot, lady, to dance
    now like a fawn who in flying   860
arcs leaps for joy, light, almost brushing the sky.
    He wins a garland of glory
greater than any Olympic victory,
your own brother; now, in the hymn strain,
praise the fair victor, chant to my step.   865

ELECTRA

O flame of day and sun's great chariot charged with light,
O earth below and dark of night where I watched before,
my eyes are clear now, I can unfold my sight to freedom,
now that Aegisthus, who had killed my father, falls.
Bring me my few belongings, what my house keeps treasured   870
as ornaments of splendor for the hair, dear friends,
for I will crown my brother as a conqueror.

CHORUS [*singing*]

                 ANTISTROPHE
Lay now the bright signs of success
    over his brow, as we circle

our chorused step, dancing to the Muses' delight.   875
    Now again in our country
our old and loved kings of the blood capture the power,
in high justice routing the unjust.
Raise to the pipe's tune shouts of our joy.

(Enter Orestes, Pylades, and servants with a corpse from the side.)

ELECTRA

O man of triumph sprung of our triumphant father   880
who fought and won below the walls of Troy—Orestes!
Take from my hands these woven bindings for your hair.
You come, a runner in no trifling race, but long
and challenging, to your home goal, killing Aegisthus
who was your enemy, who once destroyed our father.   885
    And you, companion of the shield, Pylades, son
of a most pious father, please receive your crown
from my hand, for you have won an equal share of glory
in this trial. May I see your fortune always high!

ORESTES

You must believe, Electra, that the gods have been   890
first founders of our fortune; then you may turn to praise
me as the simple servant of both god and fortune.
I come to you the killer of Aegisthus, not
in words but action. You know this, but more than this°
I have here in my hands the man himself, quite dead.   895
You may want to display him for the beasts to eat
or stick him on a stake as a toy for carrion birds
born of bright air. He's yours—once master, now slave.

ELECTRA

I am ashamed to speak and yet I wish to speak.   900

ORESTES

What is it? Speak your mind, for now you're free from fear.

ELECTRA

I am ashamed to insult the dead; some hate may strike me.

ORESTES

There is no man on earth, nor will be, who could blame you.

ELECTRA

Our city is harsh to please and takes delight in slander.

ORESTES

Speak as you need to, sister. We were joined to him   905
in bonds of hatred which could know no gentle truce.

ELECTRA

So be it.

               Which words of hatred shall I speak in prelude;
which shall I make finale, or marshal in the center?
And yet dawn after dawn I never once have missed
calling aloud what I wished to tell you to your face   910
if only I were liberated from my fears
now past. We are at that point now. I'll give you the full
torrent of abuse I hoped to tell you living.

    You ruined me, orphaned me, and him too, of a father
we loved dearly, though we had done no harm to you.   915
You bedded my mother in shame, and killed her husband
who captained the Greeks abroad while you skulked far from
    Phrygia.
You climbed such heights of stupidness that you imagined
your marriage to my mother would not marry you
to cuckoldry, though she had stained our father's bed   920
adulterously. Know this: when a man seduces another's°
wife in secret sex and then is forced to keep her,
he must be stupid if he thinks that she, unchaste
to her first husband, will suddenly turn chaste for him.

    Your household life was painful though you could not
    see it;   925
you knew in your heart that you had made a godless
    marriage,
and Mother knew she had acquired a godless husband,
so each in working evil shouldered the other's load
in mutual pain: she got your evil, you got hers.

Every time you walked outdoors in Argos, you heard   930
these words: "He's hers." And never: "She belongs to him."

O what perversion, when the woman in the house
stands out as master, not the man. I shake in hate
to see those children whom the city knows and names
not by their father's name but only by their mother's.   935
It marks the bridegroom who has climbed to a nobler bed;
when no one mentions the husband, everyone knows the
    wife.

Where you were most deceived in your grand unawareness
was your boast to be a man of power since you had money.
Wealth stays with us a little moment if at all;   940
only our characters are steadfast, not our possessions,°
for character stays with us to the end and faces
trouble, but unjust wealth dwells with poor fools but then
wings swiftly from their house after brief blossoming.

The women in your life I will not mention—a maiden   945
ought not—but only hint that I know all about them.
You took liberties since you lived in a grand palace
and were handsome enough. But let me have a husband
not girlish-faced like you but virile and well built,
whose sons would cling bold to the craggy heights of war;   950
good looks are only ornamental at the dance.

To hell with you! You know not what you did, but time
has found you out. You've paid the price. So should no
    criminal
who starts his race without a stumble vainly believe
that he has outrun Justice, till in the closing stretch   955
he nears the finish line and gains life's final goal.

CHORUS LEADER
He wrought horrors, and has paid in horror to you
and your brother. Justice has enormous power.

ELECTRA
Enough now. Servants, take his corpse into the house;

conceal it well in darkness so that when she comes   960
my mother sees no dead man till her throat is cut.

(The corpse is carried into the house.)

ORESTES°

Hold off a little; let us speak of something else.

ELECTRA

What's there? You see his men from Mycenae coming to
help?

ORESTES

Not his men. What I'm seeing is my mother who bore me.

ELECTRA

How beautifully she marches straight into our net!°   965
See how grandly she rides with chariot and finery.

ORESTES

What—what is our action now toward Mother? Do we kill
her?

ELECTRA

Don't tell me pity catches you at the sight of her.

ORESTES

O god!
How can I kill her when she bore me and brought me up?

ELECTRA

Kill her just the way she killed your father and mine.   970

ORESTES

O Phoebus, your holy word was brute and ignorant . . .

ELECTRA

Where Apollo is ignorant shall men be wise?

ORESTES

. . . that said to kill my mother, whom I must not kill.

ELECTRA

Nothing will hurt you. You are only avenging Father.

ORESTES

As matricide I'll be exiled. But I was clean before.   975

ELECTRA

Not clean before the gods, if you neglect your father.

ORESTES

I know—but will I not be punished for killing Mother?

ELECTRA

And will you not be punished for not avenging Father?

ORESTES

Did a polluted demon speak in the shape of god?

ELECTRA

Throned on the holy tripod? I shall not believe so.   980

ORESTES

And I shall not believe those oracles were pure.

ELECTRA

You must not play the coward now and fall to weakness.
Go in. I will bait her a trap as she once baited one°
which sprang at Aegisthus' touch and killed her lawful
    husband.

ORESTES

I am going in. I walk a cliff edge in a sea°   985
of evil, and evil I will do. If the gods approve,
let it be so. This game of death is bitter, not° sweet.

> (Exit Orestes and Pylades into the house. Enter Clytemnestra
> from the side in a chariot, attended by Trojan slaves.)

CHORUS [chanting]
    Hail! hail!
Queen and mistress of Argos, hail,

Tyndareus' child,
sister in blood to the lordly sons   990
of Zeus who dwell in starred and flaming
air, saviors adored by men
in the roar of the salt sea.
Hail! I honor you like the gods
for your wealth and brilliant life.   995
The time to serve° your fortunes
is now, O Queen. Hail!°

CLYTEMNESTRA

Get out of the carriage, Trojan maids; hold my hand
tight, so I can step down safely to the ground.

(They do as instructed.)

Mostly we gave the temples of our gods the spoils   1000
from Phrygia, but these girls, the best in Troy, I chose
to ornament my own house and replace the child
I lost, my loved daughter. The compensation is small.

ELECTRA

Then may not I, who am a slave and also tossed
far from my father's home to live in misery,   1005
may I not, Mother, take your most distinguished hand?

CLYTEMNESTRA

These slaves are here to help me. Do not trouble yourself.

ELECTRA

Why not? You threw me out of home like a war captive;
and with my home destroyed, then I too was destroyed,
as they are too—left dark, lonely, and fatherless.   1010

CLYTEMNESTRA

And dark and lonely were your father's plots against
those he should most have loved and least conspired to kill.
I can tell you—no. When a woman gets an evil
reputation she finds a bitter twist to her words.

This is my case now, but it is not rightly so.   1015
If you have something truly to hate, you ought to learn
the facts first; then hate is more decent. But not in the dark.

   My father Tyndareus gave me to your father's care,
not to kill me, not to kill what I bore and loved.
And yet he tempted my daughter, slyly whispering   1020
of marriage with Achilles, took her from home to Aulis
where the ships were stuck, stretched her high above the altar
and, like pale field grass, slashed Iphigenia's throat.
If this had been to save the state from siege and ruin,
if it had helped our home and spared our other children,   1025
to rack one girl for many lives—I could have forgiven.
But now for the sake of Helen's lust and for the man
who took a wife and could not punish her seducer—
for their lives' sake he took the life of my dear child.
I was unfairly wronged in this, yet not for this   1030
would I have gone so savage, nor murdered my own husband,
but he came home to me with a mad, god-filled girl
and introduced her to his bed. So there we were,
two brides being stabled in a single stall.
Oh, women are fools for sex, deny it I shall not.   1035
Since this is in our nature, when our husbands choose
to despise the bed they have, a woman is quite willing
to imitate her man and find another lover.
But then the dirty gossip puts us in the spotlight;
the guilty ones, the men, are never blamed at all.   1040
If Menelaus had been abducted from home on the sly,
should I have had to kill Orestes so my sister's
husband could be rescued? You think your father would
have borne it? Then was it fair for him to kill my child
and not be killed, while he could make me suffer so?   1045
I killed. I turned and walked the only path still open,
straight to his enemies. Would any of his friends
have helped me in the task of murder I had to do?

   Speak if you have need or reason. Refute me freely;
demonstrate how your father died without full justice.   1050

CHORUS LEADER

Justice is in your words but your justice is shameful.
A wife should give way to her husband in all things
if her mind is sound; if she refuses to see this truth
she cannot be fully counted in my reckoning.

ELECTRA

Keep in mind, Mother, those last words you spoke,   1055
giving me license to speak out freely against you.

CLYTEMNESTRA

I say them once again, child; I will not deny them.

ELECTRA

But when you hear me, Mother, will you then treat me badly?

CLYTEMNESTRA

Not so at all. I shall be glad to humor you.°

ELECTRA

Then I shall speak—and here is the keynote of my song: 1060
Mother, you who bore me, if only your mind were healthier!
Although for beauty you deserve tremendous praise,
both you and Helen, flowering from a single stalk,
you both grew foolish and have been a disgrace to Castor.
When she was abducted she walked of her own will to ruin,   1065
while you brought ruin on the finest man in Greece
and screened it with the argument that for your child
you killed your husband. The world knows you less well
    than I.
You, long before your daughter came near sacrifice,
the very hour your husband marched away from home,   1070
were setting your blond curls by the bronze mirror's light.
Now any woman who works on her beauty when her man
is gone from home indicts herself as being a whore.
She has no decent cause to show her painted face
outside the door unless she wants to look for trouble.   1075
    Of all Greek women, you were the only one I know

to hug yourself with pleasure when Troy's fortunes rose,
but when they sank, to cloud your face in sympathy.
You wanted Agamemnon never to come home.
And yet life gave you every chance to be wise and fine.   1080
You had a husband not at all worse than Aegisthus,
whom Greece herself had chosen as her king and captain;
and when your sister Helen did the things she did,
that was your time to capture glory. For black evil
is outlined clearest to our sight by the blaze of virtue.   1085

    Next. If, as you say, our father killed your daughter,
did I do any harm to you, or did my brother?
When you killed your husband, why did you not bestow
the ancestral home on us, but took to bed the gold
which never belonged to you to buy yourself a lover?   1090
And why has he not gone in exile in exchange
for your son's exile, or not have died to pay for me
who still alive have died my sister's death twice over?
If murder judges and calls for murder, I will kill
you—and your son Orestes will kill you—for Father.   1095
If the first death was just, the second too is just.
Whoever has a view to money or to birth°
and marries a bad woman is stupid: better to have
a low-born wife who's chaste than one of noble birth.

CHORUS LEADER

    It's luck determines marriage. Some seem to turn out well,   1100
    but I have seen that others have been the opposite.

CLYTEMNESTRA

    My child, from birth you always have adored your father.
    This is part of life. Some children always love
    the male; some turn more closely to their mother than to
        him.
    I know you and forgive you. I am not so happy   1105
    either, child, with what I have done or with myself.
        How poorly you look. Have you not washed? Your clothes
        are bad.°

I suppose you just got up from bed and giving birth?
     O god, how miserably my plans have all turned out.
Perhaps I drove my hate too hard against my husband.   1110

ELECTRA

Your mourning comes a little late. There is no cure.
Father is dead now. If you grieve, why not
bring back the son you sent to wander in foreign lands?

CLYTEMNESTRA

I am afraid. I have to watch my life, not his.
They say his father's death has made him very angry.   1115

ELECTRA

Why do you let your husband act like a beast against us?

CLYTEMNESTRA

That is his nature. Yours is wild and stubborn too.

ELECTRA

I was hurt. But I am going to bury my anger soon.

CLYTEMNESTRA

Good; then he never will be harsh to you again.

ELECTRA

He has been haughty; now he is staying in my house.   1120

CLYTEMNESTRA

You see? You want to blow the quarrel to new flames.

ELECTRA

I will be quiet; I fear him—the way I fear him.

CLYTEMNESTRA

Stop this talk. You called me here for something, girl.

ELECTRA

I think that you have heard that I have given birth.
Make me the proper sacrifice—I don't know how—   1125

as the law runs for children at the tenth night moon.
I have no knowledge; I have never had a child.

CLYTEMNESTRA

This is work for the woman who acted as your midwife.

ELECTRA

I acted for myself. I was alone at birth.

CLYTEMNESTRA

Your house is set so desolate of friends and neighbors?   1130

ELECTRA

No one is willing to make friends with poverty.

CLYTEMNESTRA

Then I will go and make the gods full sacrifice
as law prescribes for a child. I give you so much
grace and then pass to the meadow where my husband is,
sacrificing to the nymphs. Servants, take the wagon,   1135
set it in the stables. When you think this rite
of god draws to an end, come back to stand beside me,
for I have debts of grace to pay my husband too.

ELECTRA

Enter our poor house. And, Mother, take good care
the smoky walls put no dark stain upon your robes.   1140
Pay sacrifice to heaven as you ought to pay.

> (*Exit Clytemnestra into the house, her slaves*
> *to the side with the chariot.*)

The basket of grain is ready and the knife is sharp
which killed the bull, and close beside him you shall fall
stricken, to keep your bridal rites in the house of death
with him you slept beside in life. I give you so   1145
much grace and you shall give my father grace of justice.

> (*Exit Electra into the house.*)

CHORUS [*singing*]

STROPHE

Evils are interchanging. The winds of this house
shift now to a new track. Of old in the bath
my leader, mine, fell to his death;
the roof rang, the stone heights of the hall echoed loud   1150
to his cry: "O terrible lady, will you kill me now
newly come to my dear land at the tenth cycle of seed?"°

ANTISTROPHE

Justice circles back and brings her to judgment,   1155
she pays grief for love errant. She, when her lord
came safe home, after dragging years,
where his stone Cyclopes' walls rose straight
to the sky, there with steel
freshly honed to an edge killed him, hand on the axe. O wretched   1160
husband, whatever
suffering gripped that cruel woman:
a lioness mountain-bred, ranging out
from her oak-sheltered home, she sprang. It was done.

CLYTEMNESTRA [*singing in this brief lyrical interchange from inside*
the house while the Chorus sings in reply]

O children—by the gods—do not kill your mother—no!   1165

CHORUS

Do you hear a cry within the walls?

CLYTEMNESTRA

O, O, I am hurt—

CHORUS

I moan aloud too, to hear her in her children's hands.
Justice is given down by god soon or late;
you suffer terribly now, you acted terribly then,   1170
cruel woman, against your husband.

(Enter Orestes, Electra, and Pylades from the house, and the
corpses of Aegisthus and Clytemnestra are revealed.)

Behold them coming from the house in robes of blood
newly stained by a murdered mother, walking straight,°
living signs of triumph over her frightful cries.
There is no house, nor has there been, more suffering   1175
or pitiable than this, the house of Tantalus.

ORESTES [*singing this lyric ode in alternation with Electra and the
Chorus*]

STROPHE A

O Earth and Zeus who watch all work
men do, look at this work of blood
and corruption, two bodies in death
lying battered along the dirt°   1180
under my hands, payment
for my pain.

ELECTRA

Weep greatly, my brother, but I am to blame.
A girl burning in hatred I turned against
*   the mother who bore me.*

CHORUS

Weep for destiny; destiny yours°   1185
to mother unforgettable wrath,
to suffer unforgettable pain
beyond pain at your children's hands.
You paid for their father's death as justice asks.

ORESTES

ANTISTROPHE A

Phoebus, you hymned justice in obscure   1190
melody, but the deed has shone
white as a scar. You granted me rest
as murderers rest—to leave the land
of Greece. But where else can I go?
What state, host, god-fearing man   1195

will look steady upon my face,
who killed my mother?

ELECTRA

O weep for me. Where am I now? What dance—
what marriage may I come to? What man will take
me as bride to his bed?   1200

CHORUS

Circling, circling, your uncertain mind
veers in the blowing wind and turns;
you think piously now, but then
thoughtless you did an impious thing,
dear girl, to your brother, whose will was not with you.   1205

ORESTES

STROPHE B

You saw her agony, how she threw aside her dress,
how she was showing her breast there in the midst of death?
My god, how she bent to earth
the limbs which I was born through? and I melted!°

CHORUS

I know, I understand; you have come   1210
through grinding torment hearing her cry
so hurt, your own mother.

ORESTES

ANTISTROPHE B

She broke into a scream then, she stretched up her hand
toward my face: "My son! Oh, be pitiful, my son!"   1215
She clung to my face,
suspended, hanging; my arm dropped with the sword.

CHORUS

Unhappy woman—how could your eyes
bear to watch her blood as your own mother
fought for her breath and died there?   1220

ORESTES

I snatched a fold of my cloak to hood my eyes, and, blind,
took the sword and sacrificed
my mother—sank steel into her neck.

ELECTRA

I urged you on, I urged you on,
I touched the sword beside your hand,   1225
I worked a terrible pain and ruin.°

ORESTES°

Take it! shroud my mother's dead flesh in a cloak;
clean and close the sucking wounds.
Your own murderers were the children you bore.

ELECTRA

Behold! I wrap her close in this robe,   1230
her whom I loved and could not love,
ending our family's great disasters.

                                    (Enter the Dioscuri above the house.)

CHORUS [*now chanting*]

Whom do I see high over your house
shining in radiance? Are they hero spirits
or gods of the heavens? They are more than men   1235
in their moving. Why do they come so bright
into the eyes of mortals?

CASTOR [*speaking for both Dioscuri*]

O son of Agamemnon, hear us: we call to you,
the Twins, born with your mother, named the sons of Zeus,
I Castor, and my brother Polydeuces here.   1240
We come to Argos having turned the rolling storm
of a sea-tossed ship to quiet, when we saw the death
of this our murdered sister, your murdered mother.

Justice has claimed her, but you have not worked in justice.
As for Phoebus, Phoebus—yet he is my lord,   1245
silence. He knows what is wise, but his oracles were not wise.
Compulsion is on us all to accept this, and in future
to go complete those things which fate and Zeus assigned you.
    Give Pylades Electra as a wife in his house,
and leave Argos yourself. The city is not yours   1250
to walk in any longer, since you killed your mother.
The dreadful beast-faced goddesses of destiny
will roll you like a wheel through maddened wandering.
But when you come to Athens, fold the holy wood
of Pallas' statue to your breast—then she will check   1255
the fluttering horror of their snakes, they cannot touch you
as she holds her Gorgon-circled shield above your head.
In Athens is the Hill of Ares, where the gods
first took their seats to judge murder by public vote,
the time raw-minded Ares killed Halirrhothius   1260
in anger at his daughter's godless wedding night,
in anger at the sea lord's son. Since then this court
has been holy and trusted by both men and gods.
There you too must run the risk of trial for murder.
But the voting pebbles will be cast equal and save you;   1265
you shall not die by the verdict: Loxias will take
all blame on himself for having required your mother's
        death,
and so for the rest of time this law shall be established:
"When votes are equal the accused must have acquittal."
The dreadful goddesses, shaken in grief for this,   1270
shall go down in a crack of earth beside the Hill
to keep a dark and august oracle for men.
Then you must found a city near Arcadian
Alpheus' stream, beside the wolf god's sanctuary.
and by your name that city shall be known to men.   1275
    So much I say to you. Aegisthus' corpse the men
of Argos will hide, buried in an earth-heaped tomb.

Menelaus will bury your mother. He has come just now
to Nauplia for the first time since he captured Troy.
Helen will help him. She is home from Proteus' halls,   1280
leaving Egypt behind. She never went to Troy.
Instead, Zeus made and sent a Helen-image there
to Ilium so men might die in hate and blood.

　　So. Let Pylades take Electra, girl and wife,
and start his journey homeward, leaving Achaea's lands;   1285
let him also to his Phocian estates escort
her "husband," as they call him—set him deep in wealth.

　　Turn your feet toward Isthmus' narrow neck of earth;
make your way to the blessed hill where Cecrops dwelt.
When you have drained the fullness of this murder's doom   1290
you will again be happy, released from these distresses.

CHORUS [*chanting from now until the end of the play, like all the other*
characters]
　　Sons of Zeus, does the law allow us
　　to draw any closer toward your voice?

CASTOR
　　The law allows; you are clean of this blood.

ELECTRA
　　Will you speak to me too, Tyndarids?°   1295

CASTOR
　　Also to you. On Phoebus I place all
　　　guilt for this death.

CHORUS
　　Why could you, who are gods and brothers
　　　of the dead woman here,
　　not turn her Furies away from our halls?   1300

CASTOR
　　Fate is compelling; it leads and we follow—
　　fate and the unwise song of Apollo.

ELECTRA

And I? What Apollo, what oracle's voice
ordained I be marked in my mother's blood?

CASTOR

You shared in the act, you share in the fate: 1305
    both children a single
curse on your house has ground into dust.

ORESTES

O sister, I found you so late, and so soon
I lose you, robbed of your healing love,
and leave you behind as you leave me.   1310

CASTOR

She has a husband, she has a home, she
needs no pity, she suffers nothing
    but exile from Argos.

ELECTRA

Are there more poignant sorrows or greater
than leaving the soil of a fatherland?   1315

ORESTES

But I go too; I am forced from my father's
home; I must suffer foreigners' judgment
for the blood of my mother.

CASTOR

                                    Courage. You go
to the holy city of Pallas. Endure.   1320

ELECTRA

Hold me now closely breast against breast,
    dear brother. I love you.
But the curses bred in a mother's blood
dissolve our bonds and drive us from home.

ORESTES

   Come to me, clasp my body, lament   1325
   as if at the tomb of a man now dead.

CASTOR

   Alas, your despair rings terribly, even
      to listening gods;
   pity at mortal labor and pain still
   lives in us and the lords of heaven.   1330

ORESTES

   I shall not see you again.

ELECTRA

   I shall never more walk in the light of your eye.

ORESTES

   Now is the last I can hear your voice.

ELECTRA

   Farewell, my city.
   Many times farewell, women of my city.   1335

ORESTES

   O loyal love, do you go so soon?

ELECTRA

   I go. These tears are harsh for my eyes.

ORESTES

   Pylades, go, farewell; and be kind to   1340
      Electra in marriage.

CASTOR

   Marriage shall be their care. But the hounds
   are here. Quick, to Athens! Run to escape,
   for they hurl their ghostly tracking against you,
   serpent-fisted and blackened of flesh,   1345
   offering the fruit of terrible pain.

We two must hurry to Sicilian seas,
rescue the salt-smashed prows of the fleet.
As we move through the open valleys of air
we champion none who are stained in sin,   1350
but those who have held the holy and just
dear in their lives we will loose from harsh
    toils and save them.
So let no man be desirous of evil
nor sail with those who have broken their oaths—   1355
    as god to men I command you.

                         (Exit with Polydeuces.)

CHORUS
Farewell. The mortal who can fare well,°
not broken by trouble met on the road,
    leads a most blessed life.

                            (Exit all.)

THE TROJAN WOMEN

EURIPIDES
Translated by Richmond Lattimore

INTRODUCTION TO EURIPIDES' THE TROJAN WOMEN

The Trojan Women was part of a trilogy dealing with the general subject of the Trojan War. It was preceded by *Alexander* and *Palamedes* and followed by the satyr-play *Sisyphus*. These plays are lost. The trilogy was probably presented in 415 BCE and won the second prize.

The action of *The Trojan Women* occupies the time between the fall of Troy and the departure of the Greek fleet for home—a fleet, so the prologue tells us, which will be wrecked with much loss. The bloody and heartrending aftermath of the Trojan War—including all the episodes dramatized here—was extensively depicted in ancient Greek epic, lyric poetry, and art. At the opening of the play, all the Trojan men are dead or vanished. The women are dealt out to their future masters. The child Astyanax, son of Hector, is slaughtered "as a measure of safety." Finally, the greatest of the "Trojan Women," Troy herself, is annihilated. There is no dramatic solution, no relief. The innocent suffer. Odysseus, the villain behind the scenes, triumphs, and of the persons who appear, only the stuffy, weak-willed Spartan Menelaus and Helen, his pretty, clever, faithless, worthless Spartan wife, come out safe and sound. For despite the predictions of wreck and hardship, all readers of *The Odyssey* knew that Helen, Menelaus, and Odysseus survived to a prosperous old age.

It has often been suggested that in this play Euripides used heroic legend for the expression of his feelings about the horrors of aggressive war in his own time. For example, in 416 BCE, Athens had tried to force the neutral island state of Melos to join the Athenian confederacy. This was in peacetime. The Melians were besieged and blockaded. They capitulated, and all grown male citizens were put to death, and their women and children were enslaved. This was, however, only the most recent and most flagrant of the acts of brutality committed by both the Athenian and the Spartan sides during the ongoing hostilities of the Peloponnesian War, dating back to 431 BCE.

THE TROJAN WOMEN

Characters   POSEIDON

               ATHENA

               HECUBA, former queen of Troy

               TALTHYBIUS, herald of the Greeks

               CASSANDRA, daughter of Priam and Hecuba

               ANDROMACHE, widow of Hector

               ASTYANAX, young son of Hector and

               Andromache (silent character)

               MENELAUS, co-leader of the Greek army

               HELEN, wife of Menelaus

               CHORUS of Trojan women

*Scene: An open space before the walls of the ruined city of Troy, with
a tent that temporarily houses the captive women. As the play opens,
Hecuba is lying on the ground in front of the tent.*

                        (Enter Poseidon above the scene.)

POSEIDON

    I am Poseidon. I come from the Aegean depths
    of the sea beneath whose waters Nereid choirs evolve
    the intricate bright circle of their dancing feet.
    For since that day when Phoebus Apollo and I laid down
    on Trojan soil the close of these stone walls, drawn true   5
    and straight, there has always been affection in my heart
    unfading for these Phrygians and for their city,
    which smolders now, fallen before the Argive spears,

ruined, sacked, gutted. Such is Athena's work, and his,
the Parnassian, Epeius of Phocis, architect   10
and builder of the horse that swarmed with inward steel,
that fatal bulk which passed within the battlements,
whose fame hereafter shall be loud among men unborn,°
the wooden horse, which hid the secret spears within.
Now the gods' groves are desolate, their thrones of power   15
blood-spattered where beside the lift of the altar steps
of Zeus Defender, Priam was cut down and died.
The ships of the Achaeans load with spoils of Troy
now, the piled gold of Phrygia. And the men of Greece
who made this expedition and took the city stay   20
only for the favoring stern-wind now to greet their wives
and children after ten years' harvests wasted here.

The will of Argive Hera and Athena won
its way against my will. Between them they broke Troy.
So I must leave my altars and great Ilium,   25
since once a city sinks into sad desolation
the gods' state sickens also, and their worship fades.
Scamander's valley echoes to the wail of slaves,
the captive women given to their masters now,
some to Arcadia or the men of Thessaly   30
assigned, or to the lords of Athens, Theseus' strain;
while all the women of Troy yet unassigned are here
beneath the shelter of these walls, chosen to wait
the will of princes, and among them Tyndareus' child
Helen of Sparta, treated—rightly—as a captive slave.   35

Nearby, beside the gates, for any to look upon
who has the heart, she lies face upward, Hecuba,
weeping for multitudes her multitude of tears.
Polyxena, one daughter, even now was killed
in secrecy and pain beside Achilles' tomb.   40
Priam is gone, their children dead; one girl is left,
the maiden Cassandra, crazed by Lord Apollo's stroke,

whom Agamemnon, in despite of the gods' will
and all religion, will lead by force to his secret bed.

O city, long ago a happy place, good-bye;   45
good-bye, hewn bastions. Pallas, child of Zeus, did this.
But for her hatred, you might stand strong-founded still.

(Enter Athena above the scene.)

ATHENA

August among the gods, O vast divinity,
closest in kinship to Zeus the father of all, may one
who quarreled with you in the past make peace, and speak?   50

POSEIDON

You may, lady Athena; for the strands of kinship,
close drawn, work no small magic to enchant the mind.

ATHENA

I thank you for your gentleness, and bring you now
questions whose issue touches you and me, my lord.

POSEIDON

Is this the annunciation of some new word spoken   55
by Zeus, or any other of the divinities?

ATHENA

No; but for Troy's sake, on whose ground we stand, I come
to win the favor of your power, as my ally.

POSEIDON

You hated Troy once; did you throw your hate away
and change to pity, now its walls are black with fire?   60

ATHENA

Come back to the question. Will you take counsel with me
and help me gladly in all that I would bring to pass?

POSEIDON

I will indeed; but tell me what you wish to do.
Are you here for the Achaeans' or the Phrygians' sake?

ATHENA

For the Trojans, whom I hated this short time since,   65
to make the Achaeans' homecoming a thing of sorrow.

POSEIDON

This is a springing change of character. Why must
you hate too hard, and love too hard, your loves and hates?

ATHENA

Did you not know they outraged my temple, and shamed me?

POSEIDON

I know that Ajax dragged Cassandra thence by force.   70

ATHENA

And the Achaeans did nothing. They did not even speak.

POSEIDON

Yet they captured Ilium by your strength alone.

ATHENA

True; therefore help me. I would do some evil to them.

POSEIDON

I am ready for anything you ask. What will you do?

ATHENA

Make their home voyage a most unhappy coming home.   75

POSEIDON

While they stay here ashore, or out on the deep sea?

ATHENA

When they take ship from Ilium and set sail for home
Zeus will shower down his rainstorms and the weariless beat
of hail, to make black the bright air with roaring winds.
He has promised my hand the gift of the blazing thunderbolt   80
to dash and overwhelm with fire the Achaean ships.
Yours is your own domain, the Aegean crossing. Make
the sea thunder to the tripled wave and spinning surf,
cram thick the hollow Euboean fold with floating dead;

so after this Greeks may learn how to use with fear   85
my sacred places, and respect all gods beside.

POSEIDON

This shall be done, and joyfully. It needs no long
discourse to tell you. I will shake the Aegean Sea.
Myconos' headlands and the swine-back reefs of Delos,
the Capherean promontories, Scyros, Lemnos   90
shall take the washed-up bodies of men drowned at sea.
Back to Olympus now; gather the thunderbolts
from your father's hands, then take your watcher's post, to wait
the chance, when the Achaean fleet puts out to sea.
That mortal who sacks fallen cities is a fool   95
if he gives the temples and the tombs, the hallowed places
of the dead, to desolation. His own turn must come.

(Exit Poseidon and Athena. Hecuba rises slowly to her feet.)

HECUBA [chanting]

Rise, stricken head, from the dust;
lift up the throat. This is Troy, but Troy
and we, Troy's kings, are perished.   100
Stoop to the changing fortune.
Steer for the crossing and your fortune,
hold not life's prow on the course against
wave beat and accident.
Ah me,   105
what need I further for tears' occasion,
state perished, my sons, and my husband?
O massive pride that my fathers heaped
to magnificence, you meant nothing.
Must I be hushed? Were it better thus?   110
Should I cry a lament?
Unhappy, accursed,
limbs cramped, I lie
backed on this stiff bed.
O head, O temples   115

and sides; sweet, to shift,
let the tired spine rest,
weight eased by the sides alternate,
against the strain of the tears' song
where stricken people find music yet   120
in the song undanced of their wretchedness.

[*singing*]
You ships' prows, that the rapid
oars swept here to blessed Ilium
over the sea's blue water
and the placid harbors of Hellas   125
to the pipes' grim beat
and the swing of the shrill boat whistles;
you made the crossing, made fast ashore
the Egyptians' skill, the sea cables,
alas, by the coasts of Troy;   130
it was you, ships, that carried the fatal bride
of Menelaus, her brother Castor's shame,
the stain on the Eurotas.
Now she has killed
the sire of the fifty sons,   135
Priam; me, unhappy Hecuba,
she drove on this reef of ruin.
Such state I keep
to sit by the tents of Agamemnon.
I am led captive   140
from my house, an old, unhappy woman,
like my city ruined and pitiful.
Come then, sad wives of the Trojans
whose spears were bronze,
their daughters, brides of disaster,
let us mourn the smoke of Ilium.   145
And I, as among winged birds
the mother, lead out
the clashing cry, the song; not that song

wherein once long ago,
when Priam leaned on his scepter,   150
my feet were queens of the choir and led
the proud dance to the gods of Phrygia.

                    (Enter the First Half-Chorus from the tent.)

FIRST HALF-CHORUS [*singing this lyric interchange with Hecuba,
who continues to sing in reply*]

                         STROPHE A

Hecuba, what are these cries?
What news now? Through the tent walls
I heard your pitiful weeping,   155
and fear shivered in the breasts
of the Trojan women, who within
sob out the day of their slavery.

HECUBA

My children, the ships of the Argives
will move today. The hand is at the oar.   160

FIRST HALF-CHORUS

They will? Why? Must I take ship
so soon from the land of my fathers?

HECUBA

I know nothing. I look for disaster.

FIRST HALF-CHORUS

Alas!
Poor women of Troy, torn from your homes,   165
come, hear of miseries.
The Argives push for home.

HECUBA

Oh,
let her not come forth,
not now, my child
Cassandra, driven delirious   170
to shame us before the Argives;
not the mad one, to bring fresh pain to my pain.

Ah no.
Troy, ill-starred Troy, this is the end;
your last sad people leave you now, 175
both living and broken.

(Enter the Second Half-Chorus from the tent.)

SECOND HALF-CHORUS [*singing, while Hecuba continues to sing in reply*]

ANTISTROPHE A

Ah me. Trembling, I left the tents
of Agamemnon to listen.
Tell us, our queen. Did the Argive council
decree my death?
Or are the seamen manning the ships now, 180
oars ready for action?

HECUBA

My child, I have come stunned with terror in my soul,
awake ever since the dawn.

SECOND HALF-CHORUS

Has a herald come from the Danaans yet?
Whose wretched slave shall I be ordained? 185

HECUBA

You are near the lots now.

SECOND HALF-CHORUS

Alas!
Who will lead me away? An Argive?
To an island home? To Phthiotis?
Unhappy, surely, and far from Troy.

HECUBA

And I, 190
whose wretched slave
shall I be? Where, in my gray age,
a faint drone,
poor image of a corpse,

weak shining among dead men? Shall
I stand and keep guard at their doors,
shall I nurse their children, I who in Troy   195
held state as a princess?

(The two Half-Choruses now unite to form a single Chorus.)

CHORUS [all singing together]
STROPHE B
So pitiful, so pitiful
your shame and your lamentation.
No longer shall I move the shifting pace
of the shuttle at the looms of Ida.   200
I shall look no more on the houses of my parents.°
No more. I shall have worse troubles.
Shall I be forced to the bed of Greek masters?
I curse that night and my fortune.
Must I draw the water of Peirene,   205
a servant at sacred springs?
Might I only be taken to Athens, domain
of Theseus, the bright, the blessed!
Never to the whirl of Eurotas, not Sparta   210
detested, who gave us Helen,
not look with slave's eyes on the scourge
of Troy, Menelaus.

ANTISTROPHE B
I have heard the rumor
of the hallowed ground by Peneus,   215
bright doorstone of Olympus,
deep burdened in beauty of wealth and harvest.
There would I be next after the blessed,
the sacrosanct land of Theseus.
And they say that the land of Aetna,   220
the keep against Punic men,
mother of Sicilian mountains, sounds
in the herald's cry for games' garlands;

and the land washed
by the streaming Ionian Sea,   225
that land watered by the loveliest
of rivers, Crathis, that turns hair red-gold
and draws from the depths of sacred wells
blessings on a strong people.
[*chanting*]
See now, from the host of the Danaans   230
the herald, charged with new orders, takes
the speed of his way toward us.
What message? What command? Since we count as slaves
even now in the Dorian kingdom.

(*Talthybius enters from the side, accompanied by some soldiers.*)

TALTHYBIUS

Hecuba, incessantly my ways have led me to Troy   235
as the messenger of all the Achaean armament.
You know me from the old days, my lady; I am sent,
Talthybius, with new messages for you to hear.

HECUBA [*singing in this interchange with Talthybius, who speaks*
in reply]
It comes, beloved daughters of Troy; the thing I feared.

TALTHYBIUS

You are all given your masters now. Was this your dread?   240

HECUBA

Ah, yes. Is it Phthia, then? A city of Thessaly?
Tell me. The land of Cadmus?

TALTHYBIUS

All are allotted separately, each to a man.

HECUBA

Who is given to whom? Oh, is there any hope
left for the women of Troy?   245

TALTHYBIUS

I understand. Yet ask not for all, but for each apart.

HECUBA

Who was given my child? Tell me, who shall be lord
of my poor abused Cassandra?

TALTHYBIUS

King Agamemnon chose her. She was given to him.

HECUBA

Slave woman to that Lacedaemonian wife?
My unhappy child!   250

TALTHYBIUS

No. Rather to be joined with him in a dark bed of love.

HECUBA

She, Apollo's virgin, blessed in the privilege
the gold-haired god gave her, a life forever unwed?

TALTHYBIUS

Love's archery and the prophetic maiden struck him hard.   255

HECUBA

Dash down, my daughter,
the twigs of your consecration,
break the god's garlands to your throat gathered.

TALTHYBIUS

Is it not high favor to be brought to a king's bed?

HECUBA

And my poor youngest whom you took away,
where is she?°   260

TALTHYBIUS

You spoke now of Polyxena. Is it not so?

HECUBA

To whose arms did the lot force her?

TALTHYBIUS

She is given a guardianship, to serve Achilles' tomb.

HECUBA

To serve, my child? Over a tomb?   265
Tell me, is this their way,
some law, friend, established among the Greeks?

TALTHYBIUS

Speak of your child in words of blessing. She feels no pain.

HECUBA

What did that mean? Does she live in the sunlight still?

TALTHYBIUS

She lives her destiny, and her cares are over now.   270

HECUBA

And the wife of bronze-embattled Hector: tell me of her,
Andromache the forlorn. What shall she suffer now?

TALTHYBIUS

The son of Achilles chose her. She was given to him.

HECUBA

And I, my aged frailty crutched for support on staves,   275
whom shall I serve?

TALTHYBIUS

You shall be slave to Odysseus, lord of Ithaca.

HECUBA

Oh no, no!
Tear the shorn head,
rip nails through both cheeks.   280
Must I?
To be given as slave to serve that vile, that slippery man,
right's enemy, brute, murderous beast,
that mouth of lies and treachery, that makes void   285
faith in things promised

and turns to hate what was beloved! Oh, mourn,
daughters of Ilium, weep as one for me.
I am gone, doomed, undone,
O wretched, given 290
the worst lot of all.

CHORUS LEADER

You know your destiny now, Queen Hecuba. But mine?
What Hellene, what Achaean is my master now?

TALTHYBIUS

Men-at-arms, do your duty. Bring Cassandra forth
without delay. Our orders are to deliver her 295
to the general at once. And afterward we can bring
to the rest of the princes their allotted captive women.
But see! What is that burst of a torch flame inside?
What can it mean? Are the Trojan women setting fire
to their chambers, at point of being torn from their land 300
to sail for Argos? Have they set themselves aflame
in longing for death? I know it is the way of freedom
in times like these to stiffen the neck against disaster.
Open, there, open; let not the fate desired by these,
dreaded by the Achaeans, hurl their wrath on me. 305

(Enter Cassandra from the tent, carrying a flaming torch.)

HECUBA [*now speaking*]

You are wrong, they're not setting fires. It is my Cassandra
whirled out on running feet in the passion of her frenzy.

CASSANDRA [*singing*]

STROPHE

Lift up, heave up; carry the flame; I bring fire of worship,
torches to the temple.
Io, Hymen, my lord! Hymenaeus! 310
Blessed the bridegroom.
Blessed am I indeed to lie at a king's side,
blessed the bride of Argos.

Hymen, my lord, Hymenaeus!
Yours were the tears, my mother, 315
yours was the lamentation for my father fallen,
for your city so dear beloved,
but mine this marriage, my marriage,
and I shake out the torch flare, 320
brightness, dazzle,
light for you, Hymenaeus,
Hecate, light for you,
for the bed of virginity as man's custom ordains.

ANTISTROPHE

Let your feet dance, rippling the air; let the chorus go, 325
as when my father's fate went in blessedness.
O sacred circle of dance.
Lead now, Phoebus Apollo; I wear your laurel,
I tend your temple, 330
Hymen, O Hymenaeus!
Dance, Mother, dance, laugh; lead; let your feet
wind in the shifting pattern and follow mine,
keep the sweet step with me,
cry out the name Hymenaeus 335
and the bride's name in the shrill
and the blessed incantation.
O you daughters of Phrygia robed in splendor,
dance for my wedding,
for the husband fate appointed to lie beside me. 340

CHORUS LEADER

Can you not, Queen Hecuba, stop this bacchanal before
her light feet whirl her away into the Argive camp?

HECUBA

Fire God, in mortal marriages you lift up your torch,
but here you throw a melancholy light, not seen
through my hopes that went so high in days gone past.
    O child, 345

there never was a time I dreamed you'd wed like this,
like this, at spear's edge, under force of Argive arms.
Let me take the light; crazed, passionate, you cannot carry
it straight enough, poor child. Your fate is intemperate
as you are, always. There is no relief for you.   350

(Hecuba takes the torch from Cassandra and
gives it to some Trojan women.)

You Trojan women, take the torch inside, and change
to songs of tears this poor girl's marriage melodies.

(Exit these women with the torch into the tent.)

CASSANDRA

O Mother, star my hair with flowers of victory.
This is a king I marry; then be glad; escort   355
the bride—and if she falters, thrust her strongly on.
If Loxias lives, the Achaeans' pride, great Agamemnon
has won a wife more fatal than ever Helen was.
Since I will kill him, and avenge my brothers' blood
and my father's in the desolation of his house.   360
But I leave this in silence and sing not now the axe
to drop against my throat and other throats than mine,
the agony of the mother murdered, brought to pass
from our marriage rites, and Atreus' house made desolate.
I am ridden by god's curse still, yet I will step so far   365
out of my frenzy as to show our city's fate
is blessed beyond the Achaeans'. For one woman's sake,
one act of love, these hunted Helen down and threw
thousands of lives away. Their general—clever man—
in the name of a vile woman cut his darling down,   370
gave up for a brother the sweetness of children in his house,
all to bring back that brother's wife, a woman who went
of her free will, not caught in constraint of violence.
The Achaeans came beside Scamander's banks, and died
day after day, though none sought to wrench their land from
   them   375

nor their own towering cities. Those the war god caught
never saw their sons again, nor were they laid to rest
decently in winding sheets by their wives' hands, but lie
buried in alien ground; while all went wrong at home
as the widows perished, and couples who had raised in vain   380
their children were left childless, no one left to tend
their tombs and give to them the sacrificial blood.
For such success as this congratulate the Greeks.°
No, but the shame is better left in silence, for fear
my singing voice become the voice of wretchedness.   385
The Trojans have that glory which is loveliest:
they died for their own country. So the bodies of all
who took the spears were carried home in loving hands,
brought, in the land of their fathers, to the embrace of earth
and buried becomingly as the rite fell due. The rest,   390
those Phrygians who escaped death in battle, day by day
came home to happiness the Achaeans could not know;
their wives, their children. Then was Hector's fate so sad?
You think so. Listen to the truth. He is dead and gone
surely, but with reputation, as a valiant man.   395
How could this be, except for the Achaeans' coming?
Had they held back, none might have known how great he
    was.
The bride of Paris was the daughter of Zeus. Had he
not married her, his wife's name would sleep in endless
    silence.
Though surely the wise man will forever shrink from war,   400
yet if war come, the hero's death will lay a wreath
not lusterless on the city. The coward alone brings shame.
Let no more tears fall, Mother, for our land, nor for
this marriage I make; it is by marriage that I bring
to destruction those whom you and I have hated most.   405

CHORUS LEADER

You smile on your disasters. Can it be that you
some day will invalidate the darkness of this song?

TALTHYBIUS

    Were it not that Apollo has driven wild your wits
    I would make you sorry for sending the princes of our host
    on their way home in augury of foul speech like this.   410
    Now pride of majesty and wisdom's outward show
    have fallen to stature less than what was nothing worth
    since he, almighty prince of the assembled Hellenes,
    Atreus' son beloved, has stooped—by his own will—
    to find his love in a crazed girl. I, a plain man,   415
    would not marry this woman or keep her as my lover.
    You then, with your wits unhinged by idiocy,
    your scolding of Argos and your Trojans glorified
    I throw to the winds to scatter them. Come now with me
    to the ships, a bride—and such a bride—for Agamemnon.   420

    Hecuba, when Laertes' son calls you, be sure
    you follow; if what all say who came to Ilium
    is true, at the worst you will be a virtuous woman's slave.

CASSANDRA

    That servant is a vile thing. Oh, how can heralds keep
    their name of honor? Lackeys for despots be they, or   425
    lackeys to the people, all men must despise them still.
    You tell me that my mother must be slave in the house
    of Odysseus? Where are all Apollo's promises
    uttered to me, to my own ears, that Hecuba
    would die in Troy? What else awaits her—but enough!   430
    Poor wretch, he little dreams of what he must go through,
    when he will think Troy's pain and mine were golden grace
    beside his own luck. Ten years he spent here, and ten
    more years will follow before he at last comes home, forlorn°
    after the terror of the rock and the thin strait,   435
    Charybdis; and the mountain-striding Cyclops, who eats
    men's flesh; the Ligyan witch who changes men to swine,
    Circe; the wreck of all his ships on the salt sea,
    the lotus passion, the sacred oxen of the sun
    slaughtered, their dead flesh moaning into speech, to make   440

Odysseus listening shiver. Cut the story short:
he will go down to the water of death, and return alive
to reach his home and thousand sorrows waiting there.

Why must I hurl forth each of Odysseus' labors one by one?
Lead the way quick to the house of death where I shall take
　　my mate.　　　　　　　　　　　　　　　　　　　　445
Lord of all the sons of Danaus, haughty in your mind of
　　pride,
not by day, but evil in the evil night you shall find your grave
when I lie corpse-cold and naked next my husband's
　　sepulcher,
piled in the ditch for animals to rip and feed on, beaten by
streaming storms of winter, I who wore Apollo's sacraments.　　450
Garlands of the god I loved so well, prophetic spirit's dress,
leave me, as I leave those festivals where once I was so proud.
See, I tear your adornments from my skin not yet defiled
　　by touch,
throw them to the running winds to carry off, O lord of
　　prophecy.
Where is this general's ship, then? Lead me where I must set
　　my feet on board.　　　　　　　　　　　　　　　　455
Wait the wind of favor in the sails; yet when the ship goes out
from this shore, she carries one of the three Furies in my
　　shape.
Land of my ancestors, good-bye; O Mother, weep no more
　　for me.
You beneath the ground, my brothers, Priam, father of us all,
I will be with you soon and come triumphant to the dead
　　below,　　　　　　　　　　　　　　　　　　　　460
leaving behind me, wrecked, the house of Atreus, which
　　destroyed our house.

(Exit Cassandra escorted by Talthybius and his
soldiers to the side. Hecuba collapses.)

Handmaids of aged Hecuba, can you not see
how your mistress, powerless to cry out, lies prone? Oh, take
her hand and help her to her feet, you wretched maids.
Will you let an aged helpless woman lie so long?   465

HECUBA

No. Let me lie where I have fallen. Kind acts, my maids,
must be unkind, unwanted. All that I endure
and have endured and shall, deserves to strike me down.
O gods! What wretched things to call on—gods!—for help
although the decorous action is to invoke their aid   470
when all our hands lay hold on is unhappiness.
No. It is my pleasure first to tell good fortune's tale,
to cast its count more sadly against disasters now.
I was a princess, who was once a prince's bride,
mother by him of sons preeminent, not just   475
mere empty numbers of them, but the lords of the Phrygian
    domain,
such sons for pride to point to as not one woman ever,
no Hellene, none in the wide barbarian world might match.
And then I saw them fall before the spears of Greece,
and cut my hair for them, and laid it on their graves.   480
I mourned their father, Priam. None told me the tale
of his death. I saw it, with these eyes. I stood to watch
his throat cut, at the altar of the protecting god.
I saw my city taken. And the girls I nursed,
choice flowers to wear the pride of any husband's eyes,   485
matured to be dragged by hands of strangers from my arms.
There is no hope left that they will ever see me more,
no hope that I shall ever look on them again.
There is one more stone to key this arch of wretchedness:
I must be carried away to Hellas now, an old   490
slave woman, where all those tasks that wrack old age shall be
given me by my masters. I must work the bolt

that bars their doorway, I whose son was Hector once;
or bake their bread; lay down these withered limbs to sleep
on the bare ground, whose bed was royal once; abuse   495
this skin once delicate the slattern's way, exposed
through robes whose rags will mock my luxury of long since.
Unhappy, O unhappy! And all this came to pass
and shall be, for the way one woman chose a man.

    Cassandra, O Daughter, whose inspiration was god-shared,   500
you have paid for your consecration now; at what a price!
And you, my poor Polyxena, where are you now?
Not here, nor any boy or girl of mine, who were
so many once, is near me in my unhappiness.
And you would lift me from the ground? What hope? What
    use?   505

                        (Hecuba rises painfully.)

Guide these feet long ago so delicate in Troy,
a slave's feet now, to the straw sacks laid on the ground
and the piled stones; let me lay down my head and die
in an exhaustion of tears. Of all who walk in bliss
call not one happy yet, until the man is dead.   510

                  (Hecuba is led to the back of the stage, and
                      then falls to the ground once more.)

CHORUS [*singing*]

              STROPHE

Voice of singing, stay
with me now, for Ilium's sake;
take up the burden of tears,
new song of sorrow;
the dirge for Troy's death   515
must be chanted;
the tale of my enslavement
by the wheeled stride of the four-foot beast of the Argives,
the horse they left in the gates,
thin gold at its cheeks,   520
inward, the spears' high thunder.

Our people thronging
the rock of Troy roared out the great cry:
"The war is over! Go down,
bring this sacred wood idol   525
to the Maiden of Ilium, Zeus' daughter."
Who stayed then? Not one girl, not one
old man, in their houses,
but singing for happiness
let the lurking death in.   530

ANTISTROPHE

And the generation of Troy
swept solid to the gates
to give the goddess
her pleasure: the horse immortal, unbroken,
the nest of Argive spears,
death for the children of Dardanus   535
sealed in the sleek hill pine chamber.
In the sling of the flax twist, shipwise,
they berthed the black hull
in the shrine of Pallas Athena,   540
stone paved, washed now in the blood of our people.
Strong, joyful work
deep into black night
to the stroke of the Libyan lute
and all Troy singing, and girls'   545
light feet pulsing the air
in joyous dance measures;
indoors, lights everywhere,
torchflares on black
to forbid sleep's onset.   550

EPODE

I was there also: in the great room
I danced for the maiden of the mountains,
Artemis, Zeus' daughter.
Then the cry went up, sudden,   555

bloodshot, up and down the city, to stun
the keep of the citadel. Children
reached shivering hands to clutch
at their mother's dress.
War stalked from his hiding place.   560
Pallas did this.
Beside their altars the Trojans
died in their blood. Desolate now,
men murdered, our sleeping rooms gave up
their brides' beauty   565
to breed sons for Greek men,
sorrow for our own country.

(Enter Andromache holding Astyanax and sitting in
a wagon that comes from the side accompanied by
Greek soldiers and heaped with spoils of war.)

[chanting]
Hecuba look, I see her, rapt
to the enemy wagon, Andromache,
close to whose beating breast clings   570
the boy Astyanax, Hector's sweet child.
O carried away—to what land?—unhappy woman,
on the wagon floor, with the brazen arms
of Hector, of Troy
captive and heaped beside you,
torn now from Troy, for Achilles' son   575
to hang in the shrines of Phthia.

ANDROMACHE [singing in this lyric interchange together with
Hecuba, who sings in reply]

STROPHE A
I go at the hands of Greek masters.

HECUBA
    Alas!

ANDROMACHE
          Must the incantation . . .

HECUBA
    (Ah me!)

ANDROMACHE
                    ... of my own grief win tears from you?

HECUBA
    It must—O Zeus!

ANDROMACHE
            My own distress?   580

HECUBA
    O my children ...

ANDROMACHE
            ... once. No longer.

HECUBA
                ANTISTROPHE A
    Lost, lost, Troy our dominion ...

ANDROMACHE
    ... unhappy ...

HECUBA
            ... and my lordly children.

ANDROMACHE
    Gone, alas!

HECUBA
    They were mine.

ANDROMACHE
    Sorrows only.

HECUBA
            Sad destiny ...   585

ANDROMACHE
    ... of our city ...

HECUBA

      . . . a wreck, and burning.

ANDROMACHE

STROPHE B

Come back, O my husband.°

HECUBA

Poor child, you invoke
a dead man; my son once . . .

ANDROMACHE

. . . my defender.   590

ANDROMACHE

ANTISTROPHE B

You, who once killed the Greeks . . .

HECUBA

. . . oldest of the sons
I bore to Priam . . .

ANDROMACHE

. . . take me to my death now.

ANDROMACHE

STROPHE C

Longing for death drives deep . . .

HECUBA

     . . . O sorrowful, such is our fortune . . .   595

ANDROMACHE

. . . lost our city . . .

HECUBA

      . . . and our pain lies deep under pain piled over.

ANDROMACHE

We are the hated of the gods, since once your youngest, escaping
death, brought down Troy's towers in the arms of a worthless
   woman;

piled at the feet of Pallas the bleeding bodies of our young men
sprawled, kites' food, while Troy takes up the yoke of captivity.   600

HECUBA

ANTISTROPHE C
O my city, my city forlorn . . .

ANDROMACHE
                    . . . abandoned, I weep this . . .

HECUBA
. . . miserable last hour . . .

ANDROMACHE
                    . . . of the house where I bore my children.

HECUBA
O my sons, this city and your mother are desolate of you.
Sound of lamentation and sorrow,°
tears on tears shed. Home, farewell.   605
The dead have forgotten all sorrows.

CHORUS LEADER
They who are sad find somehow sweetness in tears, the song
of lamentation and the melancholy Muse.

ANDROMACHE [now speaking]
Hecuba, mother of the man whose spear was death   610
to the Argives, Hector: do you see what they have done to us?

HECUBA [now speaking]
I see the work of gods who pile tower-high the pride
of those who were nothing, and dash present grandeur down.

ANDROMACHE
We are carried away, sad spoils, my boy and I; our life
transformed, we who were noble have now become mere
        slaves.   615

HECUBA
Such is the terror of necessity. I lost
Cassandra, roughly torn from my arms before you came.

ANDROMACHE

Another Ajax to haunt your daughter? Some such thing
it must be. Yet you have lost still more than you yet know.

HECUBA

There is no numbering my losses. Infinitely   620
misfortune comes to outrace misfortune known before.

ANDROMACHE

Polyxena is dead. They cut your daughter's throat
to pleasure dead Achilles' corpse, above his grave.

HECUBA

O wretched. This was what Talthybius meant, that speech
cryptic, incomprehensible, yet now so clear.   625

ANDROMACHE

I saw her die, and left this wagon seat to lay
a robe upon her body and sing the threnody.

HECUBA

Poor child, poor wretched, wretched darling, sacrificed,
in pain, to a dead man. What monstrous sacrilege!

ANDROMACHE

She is dead, and this was death indeed; and yet to die   630
as she did was happier than to live as I live now.

HECUBA

Child, no. No life, no light is any kind of death,
since death is nothing, and in life the hopes live still.

ANDROMACHE

O Mother, our mother, hear me while I reason through°
this matter fairly—might it even hush your grief!   635
Death, I am sure, is like never being born, but death
is better thus by far than to live a life of pain,
since the dead, with no perception of evil, feel no grief,°
while he who was happy once and then unfortunate
finds his heart driven far from the old lost happiness.   640

She died; it is as if she never saw the light
of day, for she knows nothing now of what she suffered.
But I, who aimed the arrows of ambition high
at honor, and made them good, see now how far I fall,
I, who in Hector's house worked out all custom that brings   645
discretion's name to women. Blame them or blame them not,
there is one act that swings the scandalous speech their way
beyond all else: to leave the house and walk abroad.
I longed to do it, but put the longing aside, and stayed
always within the enclosure of my own house and court.   650
The witty speech some women cultivate I would
not practice, but kept my honest inward thought, and made
my mind my only and sufficient teacher. I gave
my lord's presence the tribute of hushed lips, and eyes
quietly downcast. I knew when my will must have its way   655
over his, knew also how to give way to him in turn.
Men learned of this; I was talked of in the Achaean camp,
and reputation has destroyed me now. At the choice
of women, Achilles' son picked me from the rest, to be
his wife: a murderer's house, and I shall be his slave.   660
If I dash back the beloved memory of Hector
and open wide my heart to my new lord, I shall be
a traitor to the dead love, and know it; if I cling
faithful to the past, I win my master's hatred. Yet
they say one night of love suffices to dissolve   665
a woman's aversion to share the bed of any man.
I hate and loathe that woman who casts away the once
beloved, and takes another in her arms of love.
Even the young mare torn from her running mate and
    teamed
with another will not easily wear the yoke. And yet   670
this is a brute and speechless beast of burden, not
like us intelligent, lower far in nature's scale.

      Dear Hector, when I had you I had a husband, great
in understanding, rank, wealth, courage: all my wish.
I was a virgin when you took me from the house   675

of my father; I gave you all my maiden love, my first,
and now you are dead, and I must cross the sea, to serve,
prisoner of war, the slave's yoke on my neck, in Greece.
No, Hecuba; can you not see my fate is worse
than hers you mourn, Polyxena's? That one thing left   680
always while life lasts, hope, is not for me. I keep
no secret deception in my heart—sweet though it be
to dream—that I shall ever be happy any more.

CHORUS LEADER

You stand where I do in misfortune, and while you mourn
your life, you tell me what I, too, am suffering.   685

HECUBA

I have never been inside the hull of a ship, but know
what I know only by hearsay and from painted scenes,
yet think that seamen, while the gale blows moderately,
take pains to spare unnecessary work, and send
one man to the steering oar, another aloft, and one   690
to pump the bilge from the hold. But when the tempest
    comes
and seas wash over the decks, they lose their nerve, and let
her go by the run at the waves' will, leaving all to chance.
So I, in this succession of disasters, swamped,
battered by this storm immortally inspired, have lost   695
my voice. I hold my tongue and let misfortune go
as it will. Yet still, beloved child, you must forget
what happened with Hector. Tears will never save you now.
Give your obedience to the new master; let your ways
entice his heart to make him love you. If you do   700
it will be better for all who are close to you. This boy,
my own son's child, might grow to manhood and bring
    back—
he alone could do it—something of our city's strength.
On some far day the children of your children might
come home, and build. There still may be another Troy.   705
But *we* say this, and others will speak also. See,

here is some runner of the Achaeans coming now.
Who is he? What news? What counsel have they taken now?

(*Enter Talthybius again from the side with his escort.*)

TALTHYBIUS

O wife of Hector, once the bravest man in Troy,
do not hate me. This is the will of the Danaans and   710
the kings. I wish I did not have to give this message.

ANDROMACHE

What can this mean, this hint of hateful things to come?

TALTHYBIUS

The council has decreed that your son—how can I say this?

ANDROMACHE

That he shall serve some other master than I serve?

TALTHYBIUS

No man of Achaea shall ever make this boy his slave.   715

ANDROMACHE

Must he be left behind in Phrygia, all alone?

TALTHYBIUS

Worse; horrible. There is no easy way to tell it.

ANDROMACHE

I thank your courtesy—unless your news be really good.

TALTHYBIUS

They will kill your son. It is monstrous. Now you know the
truth.

ANDROMACHE

Oh, this is worse than anything I heard before.   720

TALTHYBIUS

Odysseus. He urged it before the Greeks, and got his way.

ANDROMACHE

This is too much grief, and more than anyone could bear.

TALTHYBIUS

He said a hero's son could not be allowed to live.

ANDROMACHE

Even thus may his own sons some day find no mercy.

TALTHYBIUS

He must be hurled down from the battlements of Troy.   725
Let it happen this way. It will be wiser in the end.
Do not fight it. Take your grief nobly, as you were born;
give up the struggle where your strength is feebleness
with no force anywhere to help. Listen to me!
Your city is gone, your husband. You are in our power.   730
How can one woman hope to struggle against the arms
of Greece? Think, then. Give up the passionate contest.

                                                   Don't

do any shameful thing, or any deed of hatred.
And please—I request you—hurl no curse at the Achaeans
for fear the army, savage over some reckless word,   735
forbid the child his burial and the dirge of honor.
Be brave, be silent; out of such patience you'll be sure
the child you leave behind will not lie unburied here,
and that to you the Achaeans will be less unkind.

ANDROMACHE

O darling child I loved too well for happiness,   740
your enemies will kill you and leave your mother forlorn.
Your own father's nobility, where others found
protection, means your murder now. The memory
of his valor comes luckless for you. O bridal bed,
O marriage rites that brought me home to Hector's house   745
a bride, you were unhappy in the end. I lived
never thinking the baby I had was born for butchery
by Greeks, but for lordship over all Asia's pride of earth.
Poor child, are you crying too? Do you know what they
will do to you? Your fingers clutch my dress. What use,   750

to nestle like a young bird under the mother's wing?
Hector cannot come back, not burst from underground
to save you, that spear of glory caught in the quick hand,
nor Hector's kin, nor any strength of Phrygian arms.
Yours the sick leap head downward from the height, the fall 755
where none have pity, and the spirit smashed out in death.
O last and loveliest embrace of all, O child's
sweet fragrant body. Vanity in the end. I nursed
for nothing the swaddled baby at this mother's breast;
in vain the wrack of the labor pains and the long weakness. 760
Now once again, and never after this, come close
to your mother, lean against my breast and wind your arms
around my neck, and put your lips against my lips.
Greeks! Your Greek cleverness is simple barbarity.
Why kill this child, who never did you any harm? 765
O flower of the house of Tyndareus! Not his,
not Zeus' daughter, never that, but child of many fathers
I say; the daughter of Vindictiveness, of Hate,
of Blood, Death; of all wickedness that swarms on earth.
I cry it aloud: Zeus never was your father, but you 770
were born a pestilence to all Greeks and the world beside.
Accursed, who from those lovely and accursed eyes
brought down to shame and ruin the bright plains of Troy.
Oh, seize him, take him, dash him to death if it must be done;
feed on his flesh if it is your will. These are the gods 775
who damn us to this death, and I have no strength to save
my boy from execution. Cover my wretched face
and throw me into the ship and that sweet bridal bed
I walk to now across the death of my own child.

*(Talthybius lifts the child out of the wagon, which
exits to the side carrying Andromache.)*

CHORUS LEADER

Unhappy Troy! For the sweetness in one woman's arms, 780
embrace unspeakable, you lost these thousands slain.

TALTHYBIUS [*chanting*]
  Come, boy, taken from the embrace beloved
  of your mourning mother. Climb the high circle
  of the walls your fathers built. There
  end life. This was the order.   785
  Take him.

            (*He hands Astyanax to the guards, who carry him out to the side.*)

        I am not the man
  to do this. Some other
  without pity, not as I ashamed,
  should be herald of messages like this.

                                                  (*Exit to the side.*)

HECUBA [*chanting*]
  O child of my own unhappy son,   790
  shall your life be torn from your mother
  and from me? Wicked! Can I help,
  dear child, not only suffer? What help?
  Tear face, beat bosom. This is all
  my power now. O city,   795
  O child, what have we left to suffer?
  Are we not hurled
  down the whole length of disaster?

CHORUS [*singing*]
                        STROPHE A
  Telamon, O king in the land where the bees swarm,
  Salamis the surf-pounded isle where you founded your city   800
  to front that hallowed coast where Athena broke
  forth the primeval pale branch of olive,
  wreath of the bright air and a glory on Athens the shining:
  O Telamon, you came in your pride of arms
  with Alcmene's archer from Greece   805
  to Ilium, our city, to sack and destroy it
  on that age-old venture.

ANTISTROPHE A

This was the first flower of Hellenic strength Heracles brought in
    anger
for the horses promised; and by Simois' fair waters   810
checked his surf-wandering oars and made fast the ships' stern
    cables.
From those vessels came out the deadly bow hand,
death to Laomedon, as the scarlet wind of the flames swept over
masonry straight-hewn by the hands of Apollo.   815
This was a desolation of Troy
twice taken; twice in the welter of blood the walls Dardanian
went down before the red spear.

STROPHE B

In vain, then, Laomedon's child,   820
you walk in delicate pride
by the golden pitchers
in loveliest servitude
to fill Zeus' wine cups;
while Troy your mother is given to the flame to eat,   825
and the lonely beaches
mourn, as sad birds sing
for the young lost,   830
for the wives and the children
and the aged mothers.
Gone now the shining pools where you bathed,
the fields where you ran
all desolate. And you,
Ganymede, go in grace by the throne of Zeus   835
with your young, calm smile even now
as Priam's kingdom
falls to the Greek spear.   840

ANTISTROPHE B

O Love, Love, it was you
in the high halls of Dardanus,
the gods were thinking of you,

who greatly glorified Troy
on that day, binding her in marriage 845
with the gods. I speak no more
against Zeus' name.
But the light men love, that shines
through the pale wings of morning,
baleful star for this earth, 850
watched the collapse of Pergamum:
Dawn. Her lord was of this land;
she bore his children,
Tithonus, caught away by the golden car
and the starry horses, 855
who made our hopes so high.
For the gods loved Troy once.
Now they have forgotten.

(Enter Menelaus from the side, attended by soldiers.)

MENELAUS

O splendor of sunburst breaking forth this day, whereon   860
I lay my hands once more on Helen, my wife.° And yet
it is not, so much as men think, for a woman's sake
I came to Troy, but against that guest proved treacherous,   865
who like a robber carried the woman from my house.
Since the gods have seen to it that *he* paid the penalty,
fallen before the Hellenic spear, his kingdom wrecked,
I come for *her* now, the Spartan once my own, whose name
I can no longer speak with any happiness,   870
to take her away. In this house of captivity
she is numbered among the other women of Troy, a slave.
And those men whose work with the spear has won her back
gave her to me, to kill, or not to kill, but lead
alive to the land of Argos, if such be my pleasure.   875
And such it is; the death of Helen in Troy I will let
pass, have the oars take her by seaways back to Greek
soil, and there give her over to execution;

blood penalty for friends who are dead in Ilium here.
Go to the house, my followers, and take her out;   880
no, drag her out; lay hands upon that hair so stained
with men's destruction. When the winds blow fair astern
we will take ship again and bring her back to Hellas.

(*Exit several soldiers into the tent.*)

HECUBA

O power, who mount the world, wheel where the world rides,
O mystery of man's knowledge, whosoever you be,   885
named Zeus, nature's necessity or mortal mind,
I call upon you; for you walk the path none hears
yet bring all human action back to right at last.

MENELAUS

What can this mean? How strange a way to call on gods.

HECUBA

Kill your wife, Menelaus, and I will bless your name.   890
But keep your eyes away from her. Desire will win.
She looks enchantment, and where she looks homes are set
    fire;
she captures cities as she captures the eyes of men.
We have had experience, you and I. We know the truth.

(*Enter Helen from the tent escorted by soldiers.*)

HELEN

Menelaus, your first acts are argument of terror   895
to come. Your lackeys put their hands on me. I am dragged
out of my chambers by brute force. I know you hate
me; I am almost sure. And still there is one question
I would ask you, if I may. What have the Greeks decided
to do with me? Or shall I be allowed to live?   900

MENELAUS

You are not strictly condemned, but all the army gave
you into my hands, to kill you for the wrong you did me.

HELEN

> Is it permitted that I argue this, and prove
> that my death, if I am put to death, will be unjust?

MENELAUS

> I did not come to talk with you. I came to kill.   905

HECUBA

> No, Menelaus, listen to her. She should not die
> unheard. But give me leave to make the opposite case;
> the prosecution. There are things that happened in Troy
> which you know nothing of, and the long-drawn argument
> will mean her death. She never can escape us now.   910

MENELAUS

> This is a gift of leisure. Yet if she wants to speak
> she may. But it is for your sake, understand, that I give
> this privilege I never would have given for her.

HELEN   *(To Menelaus.)*

> Perhaps it will make no difference if I speak
> well or badly, and your hate will not let you answer me.   915
> All I can do is to foresee the arguments
> you will use in accusation of me, and set against
> the force of your charges, charges of my own.

> First, then!

(Pointing to Hecuba.)

> *She* mothered the beginning of all this wickedness.
> For Paris was her child. And next to her the old king,   920
> who would not destroy the infant Alexander, that dream
> of the firebrand's agony, has ruined Troy and me.
> This is not all; listen to the rest I have to say.
> Alexander was the judge of the goddess trinity.
> Pallas Athena would have given him power, to lead   925
> the Phrygian arms on Hellas and make it desolate.
> All Asia was Hera's promise, and the uttermost zones

of Europe for his lordship, if her way prevailed.
But Aphrodite, marveling at my loveliness,
promised it to him, if he would say her beauty surpassed   930
all others. Think what this means, and all the consequence.
Cypris prevailed, and I was won in marriage: all
for Greek advantage. You are not ruled by barbarians,
you have not been defeated in war nor serve a tyrant.
Yet Hellas' fortune was my own misfortune. I,   935
sold once for my body's beauty, stand accused, who should
for what has been done wear garlands on my head.

                                                 I know.

You will say all this is nothing to the immediate charge:
I did run away; I did go secretly from your house.
But when he came to me—call him any name you will: 940
Paris? or Alexander? that ruinous spirit sent
to haunt this woman—he came with a goddess at his side,
no weak one. And you—it was criminal—took ship for Crete
and left me there in Sparta in the house, alone.

                                          You see?

I wonder—and I ask this of myself, not you—   945
why *did* I do it? What made me run away from home
with the stranger, and betray my country and my hearth?
Challenge the goddess then; show your strength greater than
   Zeus'
who has the other gods in his power, and still is slave
to Aphrodite alone! Shall I not be forgiven?   950
Still you might have some show of argument against me.
When Paris was gone to the deep places of death, below
ground, and my marriage given by the gods was gone,
I should have come back to the Argive ships, left Troy.
I did try to do it, and I have witnesses,   955
the towers' gatekeepers and the sentinels on the wall,
who caught me again and again as I let down the rope
from the battlements and tried to slip away to the ground.
As for Deiphobus, my second husband: he took me away°
by force and kept me his wife against the Phrygians' will.   960

O my husband, can you kill me now and think you kill
in righteousness?° I was the bride of force. Besides,
my natural beauty brought me the sorrow of slavery
instead of victory. Would you be stronger than the gods?
Try, then. But any such ambition is absurd.   965

CHORUS LEADER

O Queen of Troy, stand by your children and your country!
Break down the beguilement of this woman, since she speaks
well, but has done wickedly. This is dangerous.

HECUBA

First, to defend the honor of the gods, and show
that the woman is a scandalous liar. I will not   970
believe it! Hera and the virgin Pallas Athena
could never be so silly and empty-headed
that Hera would sell Argos to the barbarians,
or Pallas let Athenians be the slaves of Troy.
They went to Ida in girlish emulation, vain   975
of their own loveliness? Why? Tell me the reason Hera
should fall so much in love with the idea of beauty.
To win some other lord more powerful than Zeus?
Or had Athena marked some god to be her mate,
she, whose virginity is a privilege won from Zeus,   980
she who abjures marriage? Do not trick out your own sins
by calling the gods stupid. No wise man will believe you.
You claim, and I must laugh to hear it, that Aphrodite
came at my son's side to the house of Menelaus?
She could have caught up you and your city of Amyclae   985
and set you in Ilium, moving not from the quiet of heaven!
Nonsense. My son was handsome beyond all other men.
You looked at him, and sense went Cyprian at the sight,
since Aphrodite is nothing but the human lust,
named rightly, since the word of lust begins the god's name.°   990
You saw him in the barbaric splendor of his robes,
gorgeous with gold. It made your senses itch. You thought,
being queen only in Argos, in little luxury,

that once you got rid of Sparta for the Phrygian city
where gold streamed everywhere, you could let extravagance   995
run wild. No longer were Menelaus and his house
sufficient for your spoiled luxurious appetites.
So much for that. You say my son took you away
by force. What Spartan heard you cry for help? You did
cry out? Or did you? Castor, your brother, was there, a young   1000
man, and his twin not yet caught up among the stars.
Then when you had reached Troy, and the Argives at your
    heels
came, and the agony of the murderous spears began,
when the reports came in that Menelaus' side
was winning, you would praise him, simply to make my son   1005
unhappy at the strength of his love's challenger,
forgetting your husband when the luck went back to Troy.
You worked hard: not to make yourself a better woman,
but to make sure always to be on the winning side.
You claim you tried to slip away with ropes let down   1010
from the ramparts, and this proves you stayed against your
    will?
Perhaps. But when were you ever caught in the strangling
    noose,
or sharpening a dagger? Which any noble wife
would do, desperate with longing for her lord's return.
Yet over and over again I gave you good advice: 1015
"Make your escape, my daughter; there are other girls
for my sons to marry. I will help you get away
to the ships of the Achaeans. Let the Greeks, and us,
stop fighting." So I argued, but you were not pleased.
Spoiled in the luxury of Alexander's house   1020
you liked foreigners to kiss the ground before your feet.
All that impressed you.
                                And now you dare to come outside,
figure fastidiously arranged, to look upon
the same sky as your husband, O abominable
heart, who should walk submissively in rags of robes,   1025

shivering with anxiety, head Scythian-cropped,
your old impudence gone and modesty gained at last
with reference to your sinful life.

                                       O Menelaus,
mark this, the end of my argument. Be true to your
high reputation and to Hellas. Grace both, and kill   1030
Helen. Thus make it the custom toward all womankind
hereafter, that the price of adultery is death.

CHORUS LEADER

Menelaus, keep the ancestral honor of your house.
Punish your wife, and clear your name of the accusation
of cowardice. You shall seem great even to your enemies.   1035

MENELAUS

All you have said falls into line with my own thought.
This woman left my household for a stranger's bed
of her own free will, and all this talk of Aphrodite
is for pure show. Away, and face the stones of the mob.
Atone for the long labors of the Achaeans in   1040
the brief act of dying, and know your penance for my shame.

                (Helen falls before him and embraces his knees.)

HELEN

No, by your knees! I am not guilty of the mind's
infection, which the gods sent. Do not kill! Have pity!

HECUBA

Be true to the memory of all your friends she murdered.
It is for them and for their children that I plead.   1045

                       (Menelaus pushes Helen away.)

MENELAUS

Enough, Hecuba. I am not listening to her now.
I speak to my servants: see that she is taken away
to where the ships are beached. She will make the voyage
    home.

HECUBA

But let her not be put in the same ship with you.

MENELAUS

What can you mean? That she is heavier than she was?   1050

HECUBA

A man in love once never is out of love again.

MENELAUS

Sometimes; when the beloved's heart turns false to him.
Yet it shall be as you wish. She shall not be allowed
in the same ship I sail in. This was well advised.
And once in Argos she must die the vile death earned   1055
by her vile life, and be an example to all women
to live temperately. This is not the easier way;
and yet her execution will tincture with fear
the lust of women even more depraved than she.

(Exit Menelaus and Helen to the side escorted by soldiers.)

CHORUS [singing]
                        STROPHE A
Thus, O Zeus, you betrayed all   1060
to the Achaeans: your temple
in Ilium, your misted altar,
the flame of the clotted sacraments,
the smoke of the skying incense,
Pergamum the hallowed,   1065
the ivied ravines of Ida, washed
by the running snow, the utter
peaks that surprise the sun bolts,
shining and primeval place of divinity.   1070

                    ANTISTROPHE A
Gone are your sacrifices, the choirs'
glad voices singing, for the gods
night long festivals in the dark;
gone the images, gold on wood

laid, the twelves of the sacred moons,   1075
the magic Phrygian number.
Can it be, can it be, my lord, you have forgotten,
from your throne high in heaven's
bright air, my city which is ruined
and the flame storm that broke it?   1080

STROPHE B

O my dear, my husband, O wandering ghost
unwashed, unburied; the sea hull must carry me   1085
in the flash of its wings' speed
to Argos, city of horses, where
the stone walls built by giants invade the sky.
The multitudes of our children stand
clinging to the gates and cry through their tears.
And one girl weeps:°   1090
"O Mother, the Achaeans take me away
lonely from your eyes
to the black ship
where the oars dip surf   1095
toward Salamis the blessed,
or the peak between two seas
where Pelops' castle
keeps the gates at the Isthmus."

ANTISTROPHE B

Oh that as Menelaus' ship   1100
makes way through the mid-sea
the bright pronged spear immortal of thunder might smash it
far out in the Aegean,
as in tears, in bondage to Hellas,   1105
I am cut from my country;
as she holds the golden mirror
in her hands, girls' grace,
she, Zeus' daughter.
Let him never come home again, to a room in Laconia   1110
and the hearth of his fathers;

never more to Pitana's streets
and the bronze gates of Athena;
since he possesses his shame
and the vile marriage, the sorrows 1115
of great Hellas and the land
watered by Simois.

(*Enter Talthybius again from the side, accompanied by soldiers*
who carry the body of Astyanax, laid on the shield of Hector.)

[*chanting*]
But see!
New evils multiply in our land.
Behold, O pitiful wives
of the Trojans. This is Astyanax, 1120
dead, dashed without pity from the walls, and borne
by the Danaans, who murdered him.

TALTHYBIUS
Hecuba, one last ship, that of Achilles' son,
remains, manned at the oar sweeps now, to carry back
to the shores of Phthiotis his last spoils of war. 1125
Neoptolemus himself has put to sea. He heard
news of old Peleus in difficulty and his land
invaded by Acastus, son of Pelias.
Such news put speed above all pleasure of delay.
So he is gone, and took with him Andromache, 1130
whose lamentations for her country and farewells
to Hector's tomb as she departed brought these tears
crowding into my eyes. And she implored that we
bury this dead child, your own Hector's son, who died
flung from the battlements of Troy. She asked as well 1135
that the bronze-backed shield, terror of the Achaeans once,
when the boy's father slung its defense across his side,
be not taken to the hearth of Peleus, nor the room
where the slain child's Andromache must be a bride
once more, to waken memories by its sight, but used° 1140

in place of the cedar coffin and stone-chambered tomb
for the boy's burial. He shall be laid in your arms
to wrap the body about with winding sheets, and flowers,
as well as you can, out of that which is left to you.
For she is gone. Her master's speed prevented her   1145
from giving the rites of burial to her little child.

The rest of us, once the corpse is laid out, and earth
is piled above it, must raise the mast tree, and go.
Do therefore quickly everything that you must do.
There is one labor I myself have spared you. As   1150
we forded on our way here Scamander's running water,
I washed the body and made clean the wounds. I go
now, to break ground and dig the grave for him, that my
work be made brief, as yours must be, and our tasks end
together, and the ships be put to sea, for home.   1155

HECUBA
    Lay down the circled shield of Hector on the ground:
    a hateful thing to look at; it means no love to me.

                        (*Exit Talthybius and his escort to the side.*)

    Achaeans! All your strength is in your spears, not in
    the mind. What were you afraid of, that it made you kill
    this child so savagely? That Troy, which fell, might be   1160
    raised from the ground once more? Your strength meant
        nothing, then.
    When Hector's spear was fortunate, and numberless
    strong hands were there to help him, we were still destroyed.
    Now when the city is fallen and the Phrygians slain,
    this baby terrified you? I despise the fear   1165
    which is pure terror in a mind unreasoning.

    O darling child, how wretched was this death! You might
    have fallen fighting for your city, grown to man's
    age, and married, and with the king's power like a god's,

and died happy, if there is any happiness here.   1170
But no. You grew to where you could see and learn, my child,
yet your life was not old enough to win advantage
of fortune. How wickedly, poor boy, your fathers' walls,
Apollo's handiwork, have shorn your pitiful curls
tended and trimmed to ringlets by your mother's hand,   1175
and the face she kissed once, where the brightness now is
    blood
shining through the torn bones—too horrible to say more.
O little hands, sweet likenesses of Hector's once,
now you lie broken at the wrists before my feet;
and mouth beloved whose words were once so confident,   1180
you are dead; and all was false, when you would jump into
my bed, and say: "Grandmother, when you die I will cut
my long hair in your memory, and at your grave
bring companies of boys my age, to sing farewell."
It did not happen; now I, a homeless, childless, old   1185
woman must bury your poor corpse, which is so young.
Alas for all the tendernesses, my nursing care,
and our shared slumbers gone. What would the poet say,
what words might he inscribe upon your monument?
"Here lies a little child the Argives killed, because   1190
they were afraid of him." That? The epitaph of Greek shame.
You will not win your father's heritage, except
for this, which is your coffin now: the brazen shield.

O shield, that guarded the strong shape of Hector's arm:
the bravest man of all, who wore you once, is dead.   1195
How sweet the impression of his body on your sling,
and at the true circle of your rim the stain of sweat
where in the grind of his many combats Hector leaned
his chin against you, and the drops fell from his brow!

Take up your work now; bring from what is left some fair   1200
coverings to wrap this poor dead child. The gods will not
allow us much. But let him have what we can give.

That mortal is a fool who, prospering, thinks his life
has any strong foundation; since our fortune's course
of action is the reeling way a madman takes,   1205
and no one person is ever happy all the time.

> (Hecuba's handmaidens bring out a robe and ornaments from the
> tent and help Hecuba prepare the body of Astyanax for burial.)

CHORUS LEADER
Here are your women, who bring you from the Trojan spoils
what is left, to deck the corpse for burial.

HECUBA
O child, it is not for victory in riding, won
from boys your age, not archery—in which acts our people   1210
take pride, without driving competition to excess°—
that your sire's mother lays upon you now these treasures
from what was yours before; though now the god-accursed,
Helen, has robbed you, she who has destroyed as well
the life in you, and brought to ruin all our house.   1215

CHORUS [singing in this interchange with Hecuba, who for the most
part replies speaking]
My heart,
you touched my heart, you who were once
a great lord in my city.°

HECUBA [speaking]
These Phrygian robes' magnificence you should have worn
at your marriage to some princess uttermost in pride
in all the East. I lay them on your body now.   1220
And you, once so victorious and mother of
a thousand conquests, Hector's huge beloved shield:
here is a wreath for you, who die not, yet are dead
with this body; since it is better far to honor you
than the armor of Odysseus the wicked and clever.   1225

CHORUS
Ah me.

Earth takes you, child;
our tears of sorrow.
Cry aloud, our mother.

HECUBA [*singing*]
  Yes.

CHORUS
  The dirge of the dead.

HECUBA [*singing*]
  Ah me.   1230

CHORUS
  Evils never to be forgotten.

HECUBA [*speaking*]
  I'll bind some of your wounds with bandages, and be
  your healer: a wretched one, in name alone, no use.
  Among the dead your father will take care of the others.

CHORUS
  Rip, tear your faces with hands   1235
  that beat like oars.
  Alas.

HECUBA
  Dear women. . . .

CHORUS
  Hecuba, speak to us. We are yours.° What did you cry aloud?

HECUBA
  The gods meant nothing° except to make life hard for me,   1240
  and of all cities they chose Troy to hate. In vain
  we sacrificed. And yet had not the very hand
  of a god gripped and crushed this city deep in the ground,
  we should have disappeared in darkness, and not given
  a theme for music, and the songs of men to come.   1245
  You may go now, and hide the dead in his poor tomb;
  he has those flowers that are the right of the underworld.

I think it makes small difference to the dead, if they
are buried in the tokens of luxury. All that
is an empty glorification left for those who live.   1250

(*The body of Astyanax is carried off to the side.*)

CHORUS [*singing*]
Sad mother, whose hopes were so huge
for your life. They are broken now.
Born to high blessedness
and a lordly line, child,
your death was horror.   1255

But see, see
on the high places of Ilium
the torchflares whirling in the hands
of men. For Troy
some other new agony.

(*Enter Talthybius with soldiers from the side.*)

TALTHYBIUS
I call to the captains who have orders to set fire   1260
to the city of Priam: keep no longer in the hand
the shining flame. Let loose the fire upon it. So
with the citadel of Ilium broken to the ground
we can take leave of Troy, in gladness, and go home.

I speak to you, too, for my orders include this,   1265
daughters of Troy. When the lords of the armament sound
the high echoing crash of the trumpet call, then go
to the ships of the Achaeans, to be taken away
from this land. And you, unhappiest and aged woman,
go with them. For Odysseus' men are here, to whom   1270
enslaved the lot exiles you from your native land.

HECUBA
Ah, wretched me. So this is the unhappy end
and goal of all the sorrows I have lived. I go

forth from my country and a city lit with flames.
Come, aged feet; make one last weary struggle, that I   1275
may hail my city in its affliction. O Troy, once
so huge over all Asia in the drawn wind of pride,
your very name of glory shall be stripped away.
They are burning you, and us they drag forth from our land
enslaved. O gods! Do I call upon the gods for help?   1280
We cried to them before now, and they would not hear.
Come then, hurl ourselves into the pyre. Best now
to die in the flaming ruins of our fathers' house!

TALTHYBIUS

Unhappy creature, ecstatic in your sorrows! Men,
take her, don't wait. She is Odysseus' property.   1285
You have orders to deliver her into his hands.

HECUBA [*singing, with the Chorus also singing in reply*]

STROPHE A

O sorrow.
Cronion, Zeus, lord of Phrygia,
prince of our house, have you seen
the dishonor done to the seed of Dardanus?°   1290

CHORUS

He has seen, but the great city
is a city no more, it is gone. There is no Troy.

HECUBA

ANTISTROPHE A

O sorrow.
Ilium flares.   1295
The chambers of Pergamum take fire,
the citadel and the wall's high places.

CHORUS

Our city fallen to the spear
fades as smoke winged in the sky,

halls hot in the swept fire°
and the fierce lances.

HECUBA

STROPHE B

O soil where my children grew.

CHORUS

Alas.

HECUBA

O children, hear me; it is your mother who calls.

CHORUS

They are dead you cry to. This is a dirge.

HECUBA

I lean my old body against the earth 1305
and both hands beat the ground.

CHORUS

I kneel to the earth, take up
the cry to my own dead,
poor buried husband.

HECUBA

We are taken, dragged away . . .

CHORUS

. . . a cry of pain, pain . . . 1310

HECUBA

. . . under the slave's roof . . .

CHORUS

. . . away from my country.

HECUBA

Priam, my Priam. Dead,
graveless, forlorn,
you know not what they have done to me.

CHORUS

Now dark, holy death   1315
in the brutal butchery closed his eyes.

HECUBA

ANTISTROPHE B

O gods' house, city beloved . . .

CHORUS

. . . alas . . .

HECUBA

. . . you are given the red flame and the spear's iron.

CHORUS

You will collapse to the dear ground and be nameless.

HECUBA

Ash as the skyward smoke wing   1320
piled will blot from my sight the house where I lived once.

CHORUS

Lost shall be the name of the land,
all gone, perished. Troy, city of sorrow,
is there no longer.

(A loud crash is heard.)

HECUBA

Did you see, did you hear?

CHORUS

The crash of the citadel.   1325

HECUBA

The earth shook, riven . . .

CHORUS

. . . to engulf the city.

HECUBA
O
shaking, tremulous limbs,
this is the way. Forward:
into the slave's life.

CHORUS
Mourn for the ruined city, then go away
to the ships of the Achaeans.

(Exit all.)

TEXTUAL NOTES

(The line numbers indicated are in some cases only approximate.)

THE LIBATION BEARERS

1-9: These lines are supplied from references in other Greek authors, including Aristophanes' *Frogs*, as separate quotations (1-3, 4-5a, 5b, 6-7, 8-9). The first page of the only existing manuscript of our play is missing, and it is unknown exactly how many lines have been lost or how many lines may intervene between these separate quotations.

92: The ordering of lines 92-99 is disputed. The translation here follows the order in the manuscript.

123: This line is transmitted by the manuscript as line 165 and is transposed here by modern scholars.

197: Text uncertain: possibly, "but I could know for sure to throw this strand . . ."

227-30: Scholars disagree on the proper sequence of these lines, and one line may be missing.

245: "Your" is an emendation; the manuscript reading is "be on my side"; some editors write "on our side." Some scholars assign lines 244-45 to Orestes rather than Electra.

255-263: Some editors assign these lines to Electra rather than Orestes.

285-90: The text of these lines is very uncertain.

314-509: In this long ritualized invocation of Agamemnon's spirit, the distribution of stanzas or individual verses between the chorus, Orestes, and Electra is not reliably recorded in the manuscript, and sometimes the correct assignment remains uncertain.

360: A possible alternative reading is, "you were king on earth when you lived."

375–79: Reading and interpretation very uncertain; a phrase may have dropped out.

386: Text uncertain.

415–18: Reading and sense extremely uncertain.

482: Text very uncertain, and some syllables are missing in the manuscript. Different supplements have been proposed by various editors. Some scholars have restored the text to read, "to bring death on Aegisthus and find myself a husband."

503–9: Distribution of speakers uncertain (see note on 314–509): some editors give 503–4 to Orestes, 505–7 to Electra, 508–9 to Orestes. Others delete 505–7 completely and assign 508–9 to Electra.

517: Reading uncertain.

534: Reading and sense very uncertain; some editors emend to read, "This vision would not be empty."

628: Text uncertain.

727: Reading and sense very uncertain.

785–86: Text very uncertain.

803: Two or three words are missing in the manuscript at this point.

831–36: The precise reading is uncertain in several places here, but the general sense is not in doubt.

929: The manuscript seems to assign this line ("indeed, this terror . . . clearly") to Orestes; some modern scholars prefer to attribute it to Clytaemestra.

ELECTRA

106: Another possible translation would be, "like the nightingale who has killed her child."

220: The text here is uncertain.

428–30: Some editors reject these lines as an interpolation.

451: Text and interpretation are uncertain: the manuscripts' reading means literally "nonshining."

691: An unmetrical and ungrammatical line in the manuscripts here, "the double-track race and pentathlon, as are customary," is omitted by modern editors.

720: After this the medieval manuscripts have three lines that many (but by no means all) modern editors transpose to follow line 740 instead: see the note on lines 741-43.

741-43: These three lines have been transposed here from 720-22 by several modern editors.

841-43: Text very uncertain.

1050-54: Some editors delete these lines, regarding them as interpolated.

1085-87: Text uncertain: perhaps "you have chosen a glorious life."

1264: One line is missing after this.

1283: Two or three words are missing here in the manuscripts, but the general sense is not in doubt.

1413: Text and interpretation uncertain.

1422-23: Modern editors mostly assign these lines to the chorus; the manuscripts assign them to Electra. "Blame" is also a modern conjecture, accepted by almost all editors, for the manuscripts' "speak."

1428: Two lines may be missing here, alternated between Electra and Orestes.

1458: This emendation is accepted by almost all editors, for the manuscripts' "I bid you be silent, and to reveal the doors."

1485-86: One manuscript omits these two lines, and some editors delete them.

1505-10: Some editors think these final lines have suffered damage in transmission, and that several more lines have also dropped out, leaving the ending incomplete.

IPHIGENIA AMONG THE TAURIANS

35-41: Text uncertain.

58: After this line the manuscript transmits two lines (59-60) that are rejected by most modern scholars as an interpolation: "Nor can I apply this dream to my dear ones: for Strophius did not have a son when I was being killed."

83: After this line the manuscript transmits one line (84): "which I suffered wandering throughout Greece." This line is similar to line 1455 and is deleted here by some scholars as an interpolation.

98-100: Text uncertain.

112: After this line the manuscript transmits one and a half lines (113-14) of which the text and translation are uncertain.

115: After this line the manuscript transmits two lines (116-17) which it assigns to Orestes: "We certainly did not come by ship on such a long voyage only to set out again from its limits for home." Scholars are divided whether to maintain that attribution, assign them to Pylades instead, transpose them elsewhere, or delete them.

123-25: Scholars disagree on whether to assign these first three verses to Iphigenia, to the chorus, or to both.

140: After this line the manuscript transmits one metrically defective line (141): "of the famous sons of Atreus." The correct text of these words is uncertain.

150: Text uncertain.

190-97: Text uncertain.

203: Two half-lines may be missing here.

212: After this line the manuscript transmits one line (213): "she bore, she raised, invoked by prayer." The text and meaning of this line are uncertain.

208: This line is transposed here by many scholars.

225: Text and translation uncertain.

258-59: Some scholars transpose these lines so that they come after line 245 or 335, in either case assigning them to the Herdsman.

288-90: Text uncertain.

293: After this line the manuscript transmits one line (294): "which they say the Erinyes emit as imitations." The text and meaning of this line are uncertain and many scholars reject it as an interpolation.

299: Rejected by some scholars as an interpolation.

316: After this line the manuscript transmits one line (317): "and the present disaster near to them." This line is rejected by some scholars as an interpolation.

331: The manuscript reads "stole"; the translation reflects a widely adopted modern emendation.

395: One or two words are probably missing here.

409: Text uncertain.

415: Text uncertain.

427: One word is probably missing here.

451–55: Text and translation uncertain.

515–16: These two lines are transmitted in the manuscript after line 514 and are transposed to after line 510 by many modern scholars.

571: After this line the manuscript transmits three lines (572–74): "There is much turmoil in divine affairs and in those of mortals. He feels grief in one regard only, when, although he is not stupid, he has been convinced by the words of seers and is destroyed as he is destroyed for those who know." The text and meaning of these lines is uncertain.

580: Text uncertain.

587: Text uncertain.

633: Text uncertain.

780–81: The assignment of the speakers for these lines is confused in the manuscript; the translation reflects a plausible modern scholarly correction.

798–99: These lines are assigned by the manuscript to the chorus, but most modern scholars give them to Iphigenia instead.

829: Text uncertain.

867: This line is transmitted after line 866 in the manuscript, where it is attributed to Orestes; it is transposed to after 865 and attributed to Iphigenia by modern scholars.

874: Text uncertain.

895–97: Text and translation uncertain.

907–8: Rejected by some scholars as an interpolation.

914: Text and translation uncertain.

930–36: The manuscript transmits the lines in the order indicated by the numbering; the order in which they are translated here reflects a transposition accepted by most modern scholars.

942–43: Text uncertain.

1050: This line is transmitted in the manuscript between lines 1049 and 1051 and is transposed to after line 1051 by modern scholars.

1052: This line is attributed in the manuscript to Orestes; some modern scholars assign it instead to Iphigenia.

1071: Rejected by some scholars as an interpolation.

1132–36: Text uncertain.

1143–52: Text uncertain.

1214: Iphigenia's words are missing in the manuscript.

1218: Text and translation uncertain.

1249: Text and translation uncertain.

1260: One word is probably missing in the manuscript here.

1309: Text uncertain.

1380: This word is missing in the manuscript and is supplied by modern scholars.

1469: Probably one or more lines are missing here.

1490–91: These lines are assigned to Athena by the manuscript; some scholars give them to the chorus, but it would probably be better to give them to Thoas instead. Lines 1490–96 are suspected by some scholars of being an interpolation.

1497–99: These lines are identical to *The Phoenician Women* lines 1764–66, *Orestes* 1691–93, and *Hippolytus* lines 1466a–c; most scholars reject them here as an interpolation.

ELECTRA

1: Text uncertain.

131: The manuscript reads "are you a slave"; the translation reflects a plausible modern emendation.

143–44: The text of these lines is corrupt, but their meaning is clear.

161-62: The text of these lines is very uncertain.

277: The text is corrupt but the general meaning is clear.

311: Text and meaning uncertain.

373-79: These lines are rejected by many scholars as an interpolation.

386-90: These lines are rejected by many scholars as an interpolation.

413: This phrase seems corrupt but its general sense is not in doubt.

460: Text and meaning uncertain.

484: The manuscript is corrupt here; the translation reflects a plausible modern emendation.

538: Many scholars suggest that a line has been lost in the text after this verse.

546: Text uncertain, and many scholars suggest that another line is missing after this one.

582: A line has probably been lost after this verse.

631: The manuscript reads "and I have never seen them"; the translation reflects a plausible modern emendation.

651-52: Some scholars suggest that line 651 should be rejected as an interpolation, while others suggest that it be kept but that another line has been lost in the text after it.

671-84: The assignment of verses to the individual speakers in this passage is uncertain.

682-92: The sequence, authenticity, and meaning of these lines are very uncertain.

685-89: Many scholars reject these lines as an interpolation.

832: Or "some ambush comes from abroad."

894: The text and meaning of these words are uncertain.

921-37: Some scholars suspect some of these lines of being interpolated.

941-44: Some scholars suspect these lines of being interpolated.

962-65: The manuscript assigns line 962 to Electra, 963 to Orestes, 964 to Electra, and 965 to Orestes; the translation reflects the consensus of modern scholars.

965: Many scholars suggest that a line spoken by Orestes has been lost in the text after this verse.

983–84: Text very uncertain.

985–86: Some editors emend to "I am beginning to step forward, and evil I will do."

987: The Greek manuscript reads "bitter and sweet"; the translation reflects a widely accepted modern scholarly emendation.

996: The Greek verb can mean "serve, worship, flatter, cure medically"; all these meanings are pertinent here.

997: The last words of the chorus' anapests here are corrupt.

1059: The text is uncertain but its meaning is clear.

1097–1101: These lines are rejected by most scholars as an interpolation.

1107–8: Some scholars transpose these two lines to follow line 1131.

1153: After these words, the last two lines of this strophe are missing in the manuscript.

1173: Many scholars suggest that a line has been lost in the text after this verse.

1180–82: The first of these lines is corrupt and a couple of lines have been lost after it.

1185–86: The text of these lines is uncertain.

1209: The manuscript reads "and her hair!"; the translation reflects a widely accepted modern scholarly emendation.

1226: This line is assigned to the chorus in the manuscript, but most modern scholars give it instead to Electra.

1227–29: These lines are assigned to the chorus in the manuscript, but most modern scholars give them instead to Orestes.

1295–97: Some scholars transpose these lines to follow line 1302.

1357–59: Some scholars reject these lines as an interpolation.

13-14: These two lines are rejected by most scholars as an interpolation.

201: The manuscripts read "the bodies of my sons"; the translation reflects an emendation accepted by most scholars.

261: A word or two seem to be missing here.

383-85: Some or all of these lines are rejected as interpolations by many scholars.

434: After this line, one or more verses seem to be missing; line 435 gives the probable sense.

587-94: Scholars disagree on which of these lines to assign to Hecuba, which to Andromache.

604-5: A word or two seem to be missing from each of these two lines.

634-35: These two lines are rejected by most scholars as interpolations.

638: Text uncertain.

861: After this line, the manuscripts transmit two lines, "For I am Menelaus, I who indeed have toiled much, and the Greek army" (862-63); they are rejected by most scholars as an interpolation.

959-60: These two lines are rejected by some scholars as an interpolation.

961: After this verse many scholars suggest that one or more lines have been lost.

990: The beginning of the name "Aphrodite" sounds like various Greek words for folly or lust.

1090: Text uncertain.

1140: This line is rejected by many scholars as an interpolation.

1211: Text uncertain.

1217: Astyanax's name means etymologically "lord of the city."

1239: Text uncertain.

1240: Text uncertain.

1290: Text uncertain.

1299-1300: Text uncertain.